SCHOOLS FOR OUR CITIES
urban learning in the
21st century

Richard Riddell

With a preface by Tim Brighouse

Trentham Books

Stoke on Trent, UK and Sterling, USA

Trentham Books Limited

Westview House	22883 Quicksilver Drive
734 London Road	Sterling
Oakhill	VA 20166-2012
Stoke on Trent	USA
Staffordshire	
England ST4 5NP	

First published 2003

British Library Cataloguing-in-Publication Data
A catalogue record for this book is available from the British Library

ISBN 1 85856 293 7

Designed and typeset by Trentham Print Design Ltd., Chester and printed in Great Britain by Cromwell Press Ltd., Wiltshire.

6000484700

This book is dedicated to all who work in Bristol schools and the City of Bristol local education authority

.

Contents

Preface

Is there something different and especially demanding about teaching in urban schools? And if there is, is it simply that distinction between 'urban' and 'suburban' or 'rural' or is there something more? Is the real difference about teaching well-supported youngsters in a moderately affluent and stable community, compared with youngsters whose backgrounds suffer from a possible combination of poverty, despair, violence and neglect?

The likelihood is that both are true and that issues of scale come into play. So if a school and its teachers are working with large numbers of youngsters who come from dysfunctional backgrounds, their task is significantly different and more formidably challenging than that of teachers in other settings.

In this book Richard Riddell focuses on the urban and assumes, reasonably enough, that in very large conurbations there is a demand on teachers which is different and that to meet it involves more skill, understanding and knowledge than is the case elsewhere.

'Children are the same the whole world over' is an easily repeated riposte and objection to this proposition. While true – like all simple well-worn sayings – it conceals some subtle but important qualifications. There are of course more things that are similar about teaching youngsters, whatever their age and circumstance, but there are also differences. If a child cannot see or hear or if the barriers to their learning are great then teachers have to accommodate their approach to meet the child's needs. Indeed there is a whole body of research and professional knowledge from which teachers can and do draw in such situations. But does the urban school demand different levels of general skill and even separate skill, knowledge and understanding?

I reckon there are at least two regards in which the knowledge needed is different and greater. My first teaching post illustrates their absence. In that Buxton 1960s grammar school, I knew I needed to discover as much as I could about the town and surrounding villages so that I could interlace my teaching with as many things that would arrest their attention as I could. And I could assume that in the main my youngsters arrived ready and eager to learn, from supportive and aspirational homes where whatever the levels of wealth, the unifying feature was that the youngster had been selected at eleven to enjoy what was perceived as an education which led somewhere.

Now a teacher in the inner city must set about constantly learning more and more about the many cultures which underpin the self-esteem and respect of youngsters, who come variously from a kaleidoscope of different ethnic, religious and national backgrounds. In outstanding urban teachers you see teachers whose capacity to learn and to improvise from their learning is formidable. So too is their skill in getting their youngsters ready for learning – a vital factor when the 'baggage' some bring to the school makes it a triumph of personal will over adversity that they get to school in the first place and where sometimes their parents are hostile or in-different to school. And sometimes even when they are neither of these, the school and the teacher are seen as an omni-competent helping hand in their disintegrating world of personal catastrophe. In such circumstances the teacher needs more skill, knowledge and understanding to begin to succeed in their prime task.

The author of this book started out with that assumption but as the book unfolds you will see that he has explored the issues in much greater depth and arrived at tentative conclusions which suggest the sort of curriculum and pedagogy needed if youngsters in such cir-cumstances are to have the chance of growing up into successful adults while enjoying their primary and secondary schooling.

So for two thirds of our teachers who work in urban schools and for their heads and out-of-school support staff, this book is an opener in that it touches on things which other books on urban schooling have not.

I can't resist making one of the pleas in this book by recounting a visit to a north London comprehensive school in December 2002, where I was allowed to talk with 25 pupils drawn from across the year groups and 'ask them anything you like about the school'. In the middle of it all, I asked who was the best marker of their work among the teachers. And I sat back while the most animated and informed conversation followed, as at least ten of the pupils became involved in perceptive discussion of good marking and, in particular, the value both of the marker who enabled you to see what the next stage of your learning would be and of the magic ones who told you that if you only did what they told you to do 'your work could never be excellent'. The discussion was about to end when a year 9 African-Caribbean girl observed 'The best has to be Mr Bailey my music teacher. I play the cello and sing and it doesn't matter what I do Mr Bailey has always a suggestion of how it could be better'. She paused thoughtfully before going on 'It's more than that. Mr Bailey ... He's made me see how even when he's not there how I can almost listen to my playing or my singing and know what I need to do to improve ... He calls it metacognition.' And a couple of the other pupils agreed!

Richard Riddell has opened up a debate about the importance of such practice and much else besides which those in urban settings will find useful. I hope he will be back with a sequel and that others will now focus on what really matters to the hard pressed but strong and optimistic teachers who pursue their careers where it matters most.

Tim Brighouse
Visiting Professor
Institute of Education, University of London

Acknowledgements

The concept and arguments of this book have been developing in my mind for several years now. I have been ably tutored by my former colleagues in the LEA in Bristol and the many staff whose schools and classrooms I have been privileged to visit, and in whose reflections I have shared. The book is dedicated to them.

I must also thank the city council which allowed me the opportunity of a secondment for researching and writing a book and the much-appreciated support of the DfES for doing so. In addition, I am most grateful for the welcome provided by the staff of the Faculty of Education at the University of Cambridge, where I was a Visiting Scholar for a year, especially Donald McIntyre for agreeing to have me, Angela Cutts and her colleagues in the library and Suzanne Fletcher.

Many people have contributed to my thinking over the past year as the book was developing. From Bristol they include Pat Banks, Brian Hall, Mandy Johannson, Claire Fagan, Sarah Burns, Stephen Murtagh, Ross Phillips, Ray Priest, Malcolm Brown, Nicky McAllister, Peter Scholey, Keith Sadler and Sally Boulter. Thanks also to my colleagues in the University of the West of England Richard Eke, Jo Barkham and David Johnson and to Martin Hughes at the Bristol University Graduate School of Education, all of whom gave me time and shared their insights.

Thanks are due in addition to John Coldron at Sheffield Hallam University, Karen Littleton at the Open University and Diane Reay at King's College, London for providing copies of papers and helpful comments; to Nina Franklin for easy access to NUT publications; to Carol Campbell for being able to see a pre-publication draft of

Developing Inclusive Schooling; and to Sir Peter Newsam for providing a copy of an unpublished paper and, indeed, his encouragement. They are also due to Rob Stokes, Managing Editor of the Bristol Evening Post, for being able to use the paper's archives and photographic library and to Gerry Brooke and John England for facilitating my access.

Heartfelt thanks to Louise Stoll, Geoff Whitty and Tim Brighouse for their continuing encouragement in this project this year and, as always, to Ray Shostak for his helpful and to the point observations. Above all, I must thank Andrew Pollard, who has been my mentor and critic and has rightly sent my thinking off in different directions more than once. He has enabled me to bring together a diversity of research into what I hope is a convincing story about learning disadvantage for all those who work in and with bottom strata schools.

Andrew, Geoff, Tim, Ray, Keith and Sally all made very helpful comments on the first drafts of this book – Andrew many times. I hope they will see the results of their reflections, but the responsibility is of course entirely and only mine. Many additional thanks to Tim for agreeing to write the preface and to Gillian Klein at Trentham for waiting patiently and being ever-encouraging.

The diagram of a social model of learning in chapter 5 is reproduced by kind permission of The Continuum International Publishing Group Ltd and the reflective spiral in chapter 6 by kind permission of Nicholas Brealey Publishing.

Finally, I must thank my wife Millie who continues to provide a very practical and realistic perspective for my own thinking, as well as tolerating the amount of time I have still been spending in the study, this time in order to finish the book.

Richard Riddell,
Bristol, July 2003

Chapter I
Prologue

You must be a very worried man, Mr Riddell

It is a late wintry afternoon in March, 1997. The sun, bright all day, has hardly touched the chill in the air and is now setting. Traffic is beginning to build up in preparation for the evening rush hour and the hour of evening news programmes approaches.

I am standing in a spare classroom of an inner city junior school in the poorest ward of the city. The school was rebuilt in the 1970s and is on a modern urban island, surrounded not by water, of which Bristol has plenty, but by two main roads, one of them a thoroughfare into the city centre. Changes in the relative noise levels of the traffic are easily noticed.

Just outside the school gates is one of the top so-called hotspots in the country for street crime. Drug-dealers and prostitutes can commonly be seen gathering at this time of day to catch some early evening business. Families move away from here as soon as they can and the school is forever saying goodbye to children and their parents and welcoming new ones. The head of the school has been off ill since before the previous summer and an imminent council decision is expected to amalgamate the school with its neighbouring infant school.

Nevertheless, Nina, the Acting Deputy Head, whom I have known for some years, is as always cheerful and upbeat. She has worked at the school for a long time and is well thought of by the children, their parents and her colleagues in this part of the city.

The classroom itself is growing cold; the heating has been off for some time and the children have all gone home. In the room are a sympathetic journalist and his television crew, waiting for a link to the studio. The occasion of our being here is the publication of the primary performance tables, soon after the 1996 local government reorganisation. The performance of the city's 130 primary schools was receiving public scrutiny as a group for the first time, without being buried in an alphabetical table for a large county. Nina had already been interviewed.

Sudden signs of activity show that the link is about to go live. My interview, to be included in a longer item in the evening magazine programme, was about to begin:

Journalist:	You must be a very worried man, Mr Riddell, knowing today that Bristol primary schools are among the worst in the country and that they are the worst in the South West.
RR:	Well, I don't think the tables published today do give an accurate picture of how good Bristol's primary schools are. They do not tell you what the children were able to do when they started school or what progress they have made since then. And they do a great disservice to those children for whom a Level 3, or even a 2, represents a great achievement.
Journalist:	But the results are poor aren't they?
RR:	None of us, including headteachers, think the results are good enough and we are introducing a number of initiatives in Bristol which we expect to make a difference.
Journalist:	Why are the results so poor?
RR:	Well, many schools in Bristol have high proportions of children with special educational needs – some of them over fifty percent. Many children live in straitened circumstances at home and in the community, and doing well at school for them may be the last thing on their minds.

Journalist: Teachers I interviewed today told me this too. Our viewers understand that children needing extra help with their reading and writing won't do so well, but what's being poor got to do with it?

RR: Well, as I said, it's what children bring in to school with them and what's at the front of their minds. If they have not eaten, or have come from homes which are not heated properly, or there is conflict between members of their family or in their community, it will take longer for their teachers to get the children ready for learning...

Journalist: (*Interrupting*) So you are saying, Mr Riddell, that being poor means children won't do so well in Bristol schools...?

RR: Not necessarily and certainly that isn't true for all of them. It's about the things that children worry about, how confident they feel and how well. These are the things that can make a difference in school, as I said, and to how they begin their learning each day.

Journalist: What can be done about this then and what are you and your headteachers doing which will make the results better next year? Can you tell the viewers please? You mentioned a literacy project to me earlier didn't you....?

Often told in silence

It is nine o'clock on a Monday morning and I am visiting a special school designated for children with moderate learning difficulties (though this no longer came anywhere near describing the needs of the children referred there). I am seeing the head. When I arrive, I see a small boy sitting outside his office whom I would have guessed was Year 4 (he was in fact Year 6, I learn). The head tells me he has been sent there by the class teacher because he would not speak or join in with any activity, choosing instead to sit quietly by himself.

I ring the school later in the day to speak again to the head about something else. When I ask, he tells me the boy I had seen returned to class eventually, after speaking to a Learning Support Assistant. She also happened to be one of his neighbours on the nearby local authority housing estate, and she knew his parents. He had apparently spent the weekend perched on a floor joist. It had been a cold winter so far that year and his parents had ripped up the floorboards for fuel. They had little furniture by then and school had been a comfortable relief for him. I don't ask whether he has eaten; I just know from experience that the staff at the school will ensure he does before he goes home that night.

Managing the estate

It is a Thursday afternoon and after school I am meeting the heads of a cluster of schools serving another local authority estate elsewhere in the city. This estate was notorious just then – not so much now – and one of its well-known families had just featured in the *Guardian*. An event on the estate will illustrate what I mean.

I was taking the former editor of the *Times Educational Supplement*, who was visiting Bristol at my invitation, round in my car. As we were visiting one of the primary schools on the estate which would be represented at my meeting, unbeknown to us, a major incident was taking place just down the road. A number of students from an annexe of a special school then based on the estate had gone into the local secondary school looking for someone – and for trouble. Their peers in the secondary school, or a fair number of them, decided to chase these students off their school premises, charging down the main road which ran through the middle of the estate.

As you can imagine, as many teachers as could leave the other children, and any available police officers, youth workers, social workers, behaviour support teachers, Education Welfare Officers and psychologists, rushed to the spot. Many of the students were encouraged back to school, some of them went home, but all dispersed. Luckily, there were no injuries, though a number of local residents were understandably terrified. They were visited by school staff the next day.

My meeting with the heads was to discuss behaviour support from the Authority, or rather the lack of it in their view. However, the meeting had begun informally with one of the primary heads – extremely experienced – describing what an 'awful week' his school had had. Teachers had found children almost 'out of control' every day and there had been major incidents in the playground and with parents before and after school. Attendance had been erratic for some children and was down overall, and nearly all his own time had been spent on 'fire brigade work', as he termed it, with many children spending substantial amounts of time with him in his office.

This became the only business of the meeting. As it unfolded, similar tales about the week were told by all the heads there. It confirmed their impression that things had been happening outside school to create such difficulty for them, even though their struggles and those of their staff to keep a lid on the events in school had been dominating their thoughts and actions for several days. As heads do in such situations, they shared what they had been doing and planned whom they should approach in the community and in the many external agencies based there.

The background was that at that time the estate had been going through a particularly unsettled phase with the drugs trade, with turf wars and confrontations, some of them taking place behind one of the junior schools in a road which had become notorious for trouble. There had also been a much-publicised arrest of a local minor drugs baron, following the forced entry into his reinforced council house by police and housing officers. They had smashed their way in using a JCB. Really, it was not surprising that some of the children had been affected by all this.

A tale of two cities

Now think about the child in the special school. Contrast in your mind the Monday morning for him with that of another year 6 boy I met who, that very same day, had woken up in a large detached house in another part of the city. Before going to school, he had talked to both his parents at length about their weekend trip to the countryside, where they had stayed with his uncle's family in what had become a commuter village off the M4 in Wiltshire. His parents owned their own house and both were university graduates in well-paid employment, his mother working part time.

He was shortly to be driven by his mother, along with some of his friends, to his high performing state primary school in the west of the city. In school that day, he would speak many times with his teacher about what she thought of his work, what she wanted him to do and what his thoughts about it were. The children in his class would talk in carpet time at the beginning of the day about the things they had been up to at the weekend. Our boy might be a bit 'cheeky' with the staff, especially the support staff.

In the autumn, he was anticipating going to one of the eleven independent schools in the city, whose entrance examination he had recently passed. He had already begun to discuss with his mother which university he might eventually wish to go to. They had talked about the merits of Cambridge over Oxford because he was interested in science.

From my notebooks

All these accounts are taken from my own professional experiences in Bristol, but they or others like them could be repeated in any of a thousand urban areas in the English-speaking world. And probably elsewhere besides, as many of the background themes for the work of urban educators are similar – for example, the huge range of different circumstances in which people live, urban decline in the midst of increasing prosperity, or the growth of the drugs industry and the many young people in some communities it sucks into its shadows. And these pose many similar questions for the running of urban schools – to list only a few, how we measure performance adequately and, much more importantly, how we raise it, whether all children should be taught the same things and treated the same, how long they should have to stay at school, and how they can most effectively be prepared for life as productive adults and good citizens.

This book does not provide the ultimate answers for these particular questions or another set of ready-made solutions for urban educators to take off the shelf and implement immediately. Schools are far too complex and individual for that, even when they serve the same community. What the book does do is consider where we should begin to look for answers to these questions, which is not always where we might be looking at the moment, and how schools might begin to implement them.

My argument is that the evolution of the state school system over the past generation or so, particularly in the UK, allied as it has been to economic and social change over a much longer time, has created a huge divergence in school contexts and the consequent challenges. And the disadvantage suffered by many children because of the economic and social change continues to be compounded into learning disadvantage. How this happens is explained here. Moreover, because this disadvantage arises from the very nature of learning itself, the different circumstances in which it takes place and the relations between these circumstances, any social, cultural or other distance between children and the everyday assumptions of the schools they attend also creates learning disadvantage. This can be the case even when the children are not living in poverty and are well-cared for.

In urban areas, this learning disadvantage has become particularly concentrated in certain schools and comes to characterise them. Whole communities in parts of the major conurbations are provided for by such schools, making their success doubly important and closely linked to the future success of the cities as a whole. Specifically, with the greater prosperity which has come as a result particularly of the economic upturn of the late 1990s, their success is important to ensure that all city communities may share in it and that the wealth generated is not just returned each evening to the surrounding suburbs or market towns. Success therefore has implications for social order. Finally, if these schools are not successful, neither is state education as a whole. They and their staff are on the front line of achieving high quality state education for all children.

This book is about these schools, whose success is so important to us. I call them *bottom strata schools* and consider how they have become so, what they are like, what this means for their children and what we should do there. My argument is that these schools need to provide a distinct curriculum and pedagogy, within whatever national framework prevails. This has implications for teachers and how the schools are run and led. I therefore also consider the current national framework for the work of schools in the UK and the prospects for the future success of bottom strata schools and for narrowing the gap encapsulated by our two year 6 boys. For the future well-being of their city, it is essential that they both do well.

I begin by considering the terms in which the problems faced by urban schools are described, how schools respond to them and how they are not always helpful to improvement. I call it the *crisis narrative*.

Chapter 2
The crisis narrative and its consequences

Meaning and the use of narratives

One of the ways in which human beings assign meaning and significance in their lives is by the use of narratives, which relate events to constructions of reality and which are, literally, interpretive stories or accounts of it. Many narratives come ready-made in our society and are detailed and complex from repeated use. Our lives are full of them, and we employ them not just to interpret the world but also our relations to it and to each other (Bruner, 1996).

Narratives contain thought patterns, common refrains and value assumptions. When a narrative is used to explain the significance of an event or experience, its internal logic comes into play. Conclusions and comparisons come to mind and these frame thought, speech and action. However, the assumptions and values implicit in the narrative may remain hidden, making it sometimes difficult to challenge the interpretations of reality emerging spontaneously. Narratives are very powerful.

Narratives in the public domain used about schools and the education service are very important. Parents use them to articulate their educational aspirations for their children, justify their choice of school and present their views to their children's teachers. The commentaries of politicians and the media are laced through with narratives, often similar to those used by parents.

When it comes to the staff, all these narratives co-exist or compete with their own professional ones. The interplay between them affects their enthusiasm for work and whether they think it worthwhile and that it has desirable outcomes. Their perception of whether or not they are valued as a consequence enhances or impairs their effectiveness.

The crisis narrative

Of the many narratives in the public domain about the education service, one of the most significant is the *crisis narrative*. It has been used to describe state education generally, but often refers specifically to the contribution made by urban schools. I have borrowed the term from Stephen Gorard, who discussed what he called the 'crisis account' of the education service in his book *Education and Social Justice* (2000). His intention was to show that statistically this account had no foundation, although his calculation of a segregation index has been challenged by Goldstein (2001) and Noden (2000). In any case, Gorard was talking about all schools, of which schools in cities are only a sub-set, albeit a highly stratified one, as discussed in chapter 3. And a narrative is much more than a simple account. It frames ways of thinking and the more it is heard, the easier it becomes to access and use its constructs and values.

The crisis narrative has played a dominant role in public life in the UK and elsewhere for nearly thirty years. Its central emphasis on the crisis in public education – and hence confidence – is justified by the strictures it forms about what is going wrong and the qualifications it provides to what might be going right. Depending on who is using the crisis narrative and in what connection, it is used to assign blame, call for prominent resignations or demand radical or dramatic interventions. Such is the power, dominance and pervasiveness of this narrative that it is able to construct challenges to its fulminations as 'excuses'. So much so that public discussion of urban schooling is often framed completely within its terms, even when all the protagonists to particular discussions do not believe a word of it.

Premiers, newspapers, parents and the use of the crisis narrative

Like all the major narratives concerned with education, the crisis narrative is accessed by many people. It is prominent in public life and among politicians; it is used extensively in the print and broadcast media and it can be used in different ways as a vehicle to explain a variety of actions and thoughts by parents. Children can also access it at particular times in the histories of their schools, as we shall see.

Political and public life

One of the fundamental uses of the narrative in public life is to justify change and legislative intervention. The following three quotations illustrate this. They are taken from speeches made by prime ministers or from texts to which they have put their names over thirty years.

Here is James Callaghan making his famous speech in 1976 at Ruskin College:

> I am concerned on my journeys to find complaints from industry that new recruits from schools sometimes do not have the basic tools to do the job that is required ... I have been concerned to find that many of our best trained students who have completed the higher levels of education at university or polytechnic have no desire to enter industry...There is no virtue in producing socially well adjusted members of society who are unemployed because they do not have the skills...

Callaghan was intending to initiate a great debate about education and the skills required for work. He was trying to open up the 'secret garden' of the curriculum, as it became known, that he believed to be known only to teachers. Callaghan emphasised the need for teachers' accountability (McCulloch, 2001). Although no major legislation on education reached the statute book during his term of office, his speech marked the beginning of a period of major legislative development which would dramatically affect the framework for the operation of schools and the expectations of what teachers did.

Four years after the landmark 1988 Education Act, the following passage appeared in the introduction to the 1992 White Paper, *Choice and Diversity*, over the signature of conservative Prime Minister John Major:

> ... I am not prepared to see children in some parts of this country having to settle for a second class education. Education can make or break each child's prospects.... (DfE, 1992, p iii).

Seven years later, the *Excellence in Cities* programme (DfEE, 1999a) was being launched by the new Labour government, the largest intervention ever in urban schools. The introduction to the document setting out the initiative appeared over the signatures of both the Prime Minister and the Secretary of State and said:

> ...we need a sharp, early improvement in parental confidence in the capacity of city schools to cater for ambitious and high-achieving pupils. (p1)

But the crisis narrative is not used just by prime ministers; it runs throughout the entirety of many national strategic documents, such as the last two quoted. *Excellence in Cities*, discussed in chapter 8, was a good example of an initiative which eventually was generally welcomed, but whose launch and initial documentation were coloured by apocalyptic statements drawing heavily on the crisis narrative. Here are two further examples from the same document. First:

> .....we have tolerated low standards and disruption in our classrooms, wasted individual talent and disappointed many families who aspire for their children to succeed. We have done more to express regret than we have to resolve the problems of our inner city schools.... (DfEE, 1999a, p4)

And second, in a section which gives an overview of standards in inner city areas as measured by raw performance outcomes, the document concludes:

> ...while these factors may go some way towards explaining why standards in inner cities are low, they do not justify or excuse them. And they certainly do not exempt all involved with inner city education from striving to do better. (p11)

Nothing can be clearer than that; these refrains have been common for a generation now and have formed a crucial part of the climate in which schools, particularly urban ones, have been working and trying to improve.

The media

People working in urban schools often take a jaundiced view of the 'malevolent' media (Barber, 1996a) because of their apparent predilection for bad news. With the challenges faced by all schools but particularly those in urban areas, there are many unhappinesses in the families and communities they serve, so there is no shortage of such bad news stories. The national and local media are and should be good at finding them and in situations of disagreement or dispute, it has become common for stakeholders to say they will contact the media themselves if not satisfied or if they do not achieve the outcomes they seek.

The issue is not just whether a story is carried but how. For example, '£3 million for failing schools' could describe what should be a good news story about funding for an Education Action Zone, where schools had been designing new strategies to raise achievement. 'Tables Shame' is a graphic way of describing what might be in reality a bad news story, but often one whose complexity deserves more acknowledgement than it receives.

The way stories are handled in the process means they may have few column inches and be conveyed in just a few sentences. Even longer pieces need not necessarily provide depth, but instead go for human angle interviews. So these stories need to be presented in a framework which enables the reader or viewer to recognise instantly the sort of story being unfolded and to take its intended meaning straightaway. How this is done will of course vary with the particular medium, including the editorial line, but narratives provide an ideal framework for the conveyance of instant meaning. The *ordinary person acting as a hero* narrative is typical, widely used and immediately interesting from a human point of view.

On reading, hearing or seeing a bad news story about an urban school, the consumer can be instantly drawn through appropriate narratives into a framework for understanding its significance, often starting with the headline which in effect says: 'This is another story about...' The narrative will often be the one about the *failing urban school* or, in the case of the episode with which the book began, the *bureaucrat paid large salary from public money letting children down* (in another context read 'patients'). A popular narrative in the past has been the *left wing teacher* who may also have been *politically correct* and *indoctrinating our children*. This is even worse when it has gone on *behind our backs.*

The media are the most important public vehicle for the expression of the views of all active participants in public life, particularly politicians, and are often the only means by which their views receive a public airing on a regular basis, even during elections. This does not mean the media are always the vehicle politicians would like. Nevertheless, politicians' use of the crisis narrative becomes significant in this way, entering the public consciousness for recycling and further reference, possibly reinforced by the nature of the coverage and its related editorials.

The media do not have to use the crisis narrative any more than do politicians and can promote something different. Sometimes they do. Either way, the choice they make is significant and affects the subject of their attention.

Parents
With the crisis narrative being such an important part of public life and being used by the media at least some of the time, it is not surprising that parents use it too. Parents, like all of us, can be influenced by the narratives they use, but they also bear concerns which they genuinely feel. That is why they use the crisis narrative in the first place and it explains how it has been picked up in the public fulminations of the past thirty years. This is not necessarily a cynical process. The 'anxious but formidable north London parent', for example, who is 'absolutely committed to a good education for their children but (does) not expect to find it in their local comprehensive', described by Barber (1996a, p111), is obviously not an invention of politicians or the media. The profound economic and social change in the UK and elsewhere has influenced the way that many parents think as well as speak, and not just in London.

Like all narratives, the crisis narrative has multiple uses. Concern arises for all public services, however, when it is used by key stakeholders as they respond to its indiscriminate use in public life or the media, and its very use then crystallises concerns which may be without foundation. Such use may then precipitate a real crisis because of the loss of confidence engendered.

Occasionally for a school there is an apocalyptic confluence in the dramatically expressed opinions of politicians, the media and parents. Cameras can keep appearing outside the school gates in support of damaging stories following a particular decision by a headteacher. If this is followed by parental flight from the school, the damage is hard to stem. It is easy to see how a siege mentality sets in and the views of staff of their own worth and work can change, however powerful their professional narratives. It is this dynamic that becomes the real crisis for the school, and staff begin to lose the confidence to do anything about it.

Opportunities for use of the crisis narrative

The national framework of policies which govern the education service in the UK, with their emphasis on performance and public accountability, offer many opportunities for the use of the crisis narrative in addition to the human interest stories. By the nature of things, these opportunities often arise in connection with urban schools.

One of these opportunities is the annual publication of the performance tables. The tables compare performance at the age of 11, 14, 16 and 18 broadly on an unadjusted basis, although value added measures have recently been applied to progress from 11 to 14 and from 14 to16. Because of the nature of the tables, the schools and their local education authorities which cluster around the bottom are, with a few outstanding exceptions, those with the highest deprivation statistics or – which often amounts to the same thing – those in urban areas. As Power *et al* (2002) note: 'Research supports the commonly held assumption that it is inner-city schools whose performance is weakest'. The original *Excellence in Cities* prospectus (DfEE, 1999a) highlighted the comparatively low achievement of five A*-C grades at GCSE in inner city secondary schools of 33per cent against 46per cent achieved nationally.

Now, irrespective of their rate of improvement, even when it is faster than that of schools in more advantaged areas, urban (and other) schools at the bottom of the tables await their 'tables shame' headlines every year, sometimes with damaging effects. This annual narrative seems difficult to resist in the local and national media (for example, in illustrating the 'best and worst schools by region'). And, no matter the value added scores and other sophisticated data, even when they are in the public domain, parents will in reality almost invariably consider the schools with higher scores to be the better ones – which was the tables' purpose. The tones of the crisis narrative merely add weight to their beliefs.

The crisis narrative is used multiply here: by the media to describe the situation signified by the tables and by those in public life, usually politicians, to describe the bold action already taken in anticipation or as a consequence. This is when the narrative might be picked up by some parents to strengthen their convictions about choice of school or create the impression in others that they need to move their children as soon as possible. The publication of the tables invites use of the crisis narrative in connection with certain schools, very often urban ones, and is used at all levels to accompany market pressure.

The publication of poor inspection reports following an Ofsted inspection provides similar fodder for the crisis narrative. The legitimacy or soundness of the verdicts passed on schools by inspection is not being questioned here, although some would challenge the basis for them. Nor should schools escape attention which are not providing adequately for their children. It is the vivid use of the crisis narrative in presentations of the published report which is questionable. These impair the capacity of the schools targeted to improve, schools that are often particularly vulnerable in the first place thanks to the comparisons made with national attainment.

The starkness of such public descriptions often affects the children and the way they think about themselves – self-confidence is a key theme for learning (see chapter 4) – so this does not help. Many experiences of this have been documented nationally, but one of the most vivid for me was in a primary school in Bristol. In assembly, the day after the publication of the school's inspection report, the older children anxiously asked the headteacher whether they could read or write. They had thought they could, but standards of literacy had been roundly criticised in the school's inspection report, in a manner characteristic of the early years of Ofsted, and this had received extensive media coverage.

Concerns identified in the performance tables or by Ofsted inspections point up the need for action and the changing policies for responding to school failure have provided further opportunities for use of the crisis narrative. The need for such policies was much discussed in the mid-1990s – Michael Barber, for example, devoted his *TES*/Greenwich Lecture in 1995 to ending failure in urban education, as he put it (see his updated version in Stoll and Myers, 1998). Significant agreement emerged that schools do sometimes lose their capacity to improve, so requiring intervention. If a school was found to have serious weaknesses after inspection, for example, or not to be providing an adequate standard of education, specific regimes came to be required from the school and local education authority (the 'special measures'), and regular inspection visits continued (DfEE, 1998a). As the policies developed, local education authorities were required to have their own policies for dealing with schools causing them concern and these were to be governed by a national code of practice (DfEE, 1998b) developed for the purpose. As far as these went, these policies and interventions were clearly sensible and necessary.

But surely a better balance could have been achieved between the measures required for schools which had lost their capacity and their dramatic public representations. Instead, matters were often made worse in the schools concerned by the use of the crisis narrative, reducing their capacity further, undermining their professional and sometimes personal self-confidence and making recovery harder. And the sense of crisis often spread rapidly in urban areas, as colleagues in nearby schools watched anxiously to see how events unfolded, how intervention was managed and who the casualties were to be.

It is hard not to believe that the language of special measures, serious weaknesses and the compulsory condign responses was not intentionally designed to demoralise. Just read the dramatic terms in which the original DfEE document (1998a) presented the consequences of inspection, the need for intervention and the so-called 'fresh start' regime in response to poor performance. 'Failure' is a loaded word in the crisis narrative and has particularly destructive tones for heads and teachers.

The nature of the intervention required in schools at the bottom of their trajectories will continue to be discussed. Although the numbers of schools requiring special measures have declined for some years (Ofsted, 2002; Blunkett, 2000a), and more schools have been coming out of special measures quicker, the processes of bringing them out have been complex. Schools which no longer qualify for the category have not all suddenly become successful (Stoll and Myers, 1998). The inspection judgement made about them was whether they could become so under their own steam. There have been celebrated cases of schools whose performance was not high or even improving, several years after coming out of special measures and despite nationally-recognised 'good leadership'.

This was the background to the launch of the *Schools Facing Challenging Circumstances* scheme, following the announcement of the measures for *Transforming Secondary Education* (Blunkett, 2000b), discussed in Chapter 8. Schools were identified for the scheme on the basis of the Secretary of State's minimum aspiration that 20 per cent of children in all secondary schools should be achieving five GCSE grades at A* to C by 2004 and that this should rise to 25 per cent by 2006.

The scheme provides another illustration of how what might be seen as sensible measures can be described in stark crisis terms, affecting how they are received by the very people who have to implement them – the staff in the schools. Leaving aside how the resources were targeted and the bureaucratic aspects of the requirements on schools, it was essential that the schools received support. When facing multiple disadvantage, it is important that the difficulties experienced in raising achievement are recognised, that there is effective national networking and that attempts are made to build the schools' capacity to improve. The launch of the scheme to headteachers at a national conference in December 2000 was as unfortunate as that for Excellence in Cities, as the focus was restricted to raw performance issues, presented in the stark terms of the crisis narrative.

According to the DfEE *Handbook of Guidance* for schools in the scheme (Hopkins *et al,* 2001), of the 620 secondary schools originally identified for support (out of some 5,000 secondary schools in England and Wales), the average level of free school meals was 36 per cent (against a national average of about 20%), but the highest figure was 84%. So again, the schools qualifying for the scheme were likely to be in areas suffering from deprivation and mostly therefore in urban areas. All will fall within the definition of 'bottom strata schools'. Sadly, even when the support is real, as it is, and the tone constructive, as it certainly became, the language and trappings of the scheme itself can heighten the sense of crisis in the schools. 'Crisis' and 'urban' again become synonymous.

Are there alternatives to the crisis narrative?
Staff in urban schools would rather not see the quality of their work described in terms of the crisis narrative. Yet, should a real crisis not be acknowledged? The Prime Minister's speech to the 2002 labour party conference (Blair, 2002) suggested there was still a general crisis in aspects of the public services and that, after more than five years in government, the party, government and country were at a 'crossroads'.

The question is not whether things are acknowledged, but how. Some of the weaknesses highlighted in Ofsted inspections have been serious. Inspection findings have sometimes confirmed what was suspected and said by governors, parents, local politicians or local authority officers, but remained unacknowledged locally or even resisted. Sometimes the findings have been a revelation. That change and improvement were needed in some schools could not be gainsaid and there was justification for change, sometimes dramatic, on a national scale.

This is still true. In addition, schools do not remain either 'good' or 'bad' indefinitely (Stoll and Fink, 1995); they are always changing. They need to be vigilant and they should be monitored. There are still dramatic performance differences between schools serving apparently similar communities and between children with apparently similar characteristics. Parents still worry about the schools their children are expected to attend, particularly at secondary level, and this cannot be ignored.

But the crisis narrative, to labour the point, although deliberately intended to increase pressure for change, may create a crisis where none existed before, undermine confidence in public services and reduce the capacity of staff who need to make the required changes. That things need to improve does not mean there is a crisis. Sometimes the staff concerned are not able to make the changes needed, but the ability of those who can or could make the effective change is endangered. The crisis narrative makes it more difficult for teachers in the spotlight to accept that things must change, that it is their responsibility to ensure they do, and that they have made mistakes. It is hard for staff dispassionately to analyse, reflect and create the changes needed and easier for them to make 'excuses' within the crisis narrative's own terms.

Before responsibility for improvement can be accepted openly and willingly, and achieved effectively, a different national climate is needed, one that allows for frank and open discussion about performance and improving it, free of the discourse of crisis and personal blame. Public discussion of public services needs to be conducted in a responsible manner, not as a drama. This is down to everyone, not just politicians, although those in public life should lead by example. Whether the discourse is becoming more constructive is discussed in chapter 9.

One last point: the establishment of a constructive public climate is essential to the tasks of reducing inequalities in educational outcome, countering learning disadvantage and achieving social justice. The diagnosis may have been correct, but not the cure. In many communities, the complexity of what bottom strata schools have to deal with is too often underestimated, because the complexity of the learning process is not understood. The issue of urban learning is the core of this book.

An accurate picture of how bottom strata schools may effectively counter learning disadvantage is a complicated jigsaw. I begin assembling this jigsaw by considering how bottom strata schools have emerged.

Chapter 3

Stratification and the emergence
of bottom strata schools
in urban areas

Economic and Social Change since the Second World War

The schools that are the focus of this book have been shaped by a progression of complex processes over the past fifty years. Economic and social change has been reflected in political and legislative reform. Views about lifestyle have altered and parents' aspirations for their children have found new and different forms.

To understand how bottom strata schools have emerged, we need to understand how a larger middle class has evolved, and examine its desire to pass on social and cultural capital to its children against the background of credential inflation. The development of the subjective reality of parental aspiration is as relevant and significant as the objective reality of wider societal change.

The post-modern era of globalisation in which we now live began, by the conventional understanding of economic history, in 1973 when the oil crisis of that year was followed by a world recession. There have been many accounts of these events and their importance, such as Brown and Lauder (1997):

> Since the first oil shock in the early 1970s, western societies have experienced a social, political and economic transformation that is yet to reach its conclusion. At its epicentre is the creation of a global economy

that has led to an intensification of competition between firms, regions and nation states. (p172)

The dramatic period of recession and high inflation in the 1970s had followed a prolonged period of unprecedented growth. Output in the developed countries was 180 per cent higher in 1973 than in 1950 and people from a wide social spectrum had shared in increasing prosperity in a way they did not in the economic hardship which set in after 1973.

After the Second World War, the rising prosperity in the UK, accompanied by a redistributive tax system, helped bring about many social changes. Provision by the welfare state grew dramatically. There was universal secondary education, access to higher education by working class children reached the highest for a generation, aided by student grants, and the gap between the richest and the poorest in society narrowed (Power *et al,* 2002). There was an expectation that prosperity would continue, fuelled, it was believed, by the 'white heat of technology', in Harold Wilson's much misquoted phrase.

The expanding state bureaucracies and the white collar requirements of large industrial concerns led to a growth in 'middle class' jobs, which, until the 1970s, were stable. Investment in education was widely considered essential to maintain national economic growth and prosperity, and in personal terms, access to educational opportunities to seek better qualifications (so-called credential inflation) was considered essential. Prosperity was measured by the middle class in terms of the possession of consumer goods and durables, including cars, and home ownership secured on the basis of borrowing at low interest rates. The consumer economy began to generate its own values and expectations about lifestyle.

Education, therefore, was a positional good and was seen in this light. It was the route to social as well as economic betterment. Jackson (1964) documents such expectations on the part of parents, while showing that schools were making early structural decisions about certain children which limited the real options for their futures. Even so, and even with the resistance to school developed by many working class children (Jackson and Marsden, 1962), the educational limitations seemed less important because men could opt for the 'physically tough' jobs which did not require qualifications (Halsey *et al*, 1997, p11). The other alternative of the traditional craft apprenticeship enabled a traditional and disciplined socialisation into the adult world.

The major recession that began in the 1970s changed all this. It accelerated the economic restructuring in the developed economies, begun long before, whereby traditional industrial and manufacturing bases shrank enormously in employment terms or disappeared altogether. Restructurings had often been seen as a natural part of the economic cycle, but the 1970s recession was the most fundamental since the war in its effects.

By then it had become commonplace for home-produced manufactured goods to be undercut by imports from other countries, often the newly industrialised ones which had lower labour costs after a generation of wage inflation in the west. Manufacturers in the developed countries and companies involved in information processing began to look globally for lower costs, often taking advantage of short term local subsidies.

This had major effects on the UK's industrial cities, with social effects following shortly behind economic ones. Cities in the north and midlands were particularly affected, but the phenomenon itself was worldwide and was felt in all the developed countries. As Pat Thomson describes it:

> The global rustbelt trails round the United Kingdom, through parts of Europe, Canada and the United States, and through Australia and New Zealand ... (It is) an indelible blemish on the economic complexion of some of the wealthiest countries in the world. (2002, p26)

Unemployment in the UK, already increasing in the early 1970s, reached record levels in the 1980s under the harsh economic policies of the government in power, which continued for some time:

> Rising unemployment and the recession have been the price we have had to pay to get inflation down. (Labour shouts) That is a price well-worth paying. (Norman Lamont in a speech in the House of Commons, Hansard, 16 May 1991)

By the early 1980s there was mass youth unemployment, helping to shape expectations for a whole generation about work, prosperity, gender roles, education and much else. The 1991 Census documented the scale of the social and economic change which had been taking place in UK cities. Although another turn in the economic cycle during the 1990s brought recovery, it did not benefit all the communities hardest hit by the previous recessions.

On predominantly blue collar estates, ie local authority housing estates built largely since the war, employment collapsed as the local large employers disappeared or downsized. It proved difficult to re-suscitate employment in these areas by developing the new indus-trial estates of predominantly small-scale units, or by attracting high tech industry. The landscape of work on the estates had changed for ever.

The disappearance or downsizing of the large scale employers and widespread cuts in public expenditure also changed employment prospects in the white collar bureaucracies during the 1980s, in both the private and public sectors. This caused greater insecurity among the middle class, now a third of the population (Roberts, 2001). They experienced redundancies for the first time, which explains the later growth in self-employment and small business.

British society in the 1960s was by no means classless or without social divisions, but the divisions became more severe in the after-math of the economic changes of the 1970s, as income gaps began to grow once again (Power *et al,* 2002). By the 1990s, the social and economic spectrum was very wide and the divide continues despite the effects of Labour's initiative of the working family tax credit.

At one end of the spectrum were the blue collar estates and other urban areas. They became the object of the policies of national and local government, most recently the Neighbourhood Renewal Strategy (Social Exclusion Unit, 2001). The end of reliable work for so many families in urban communities meant increasing poverty, social dissolution and community breakdown in the worst cases, the rise of drug abuse and crime generating an alternative set of expecta-tions and aspirations for too many young people. The presence in schools of the children of second, or even third, generation un-employed families in the 1980s and 1990s, which had no experience of work routine or discipline, or had forgotten it, presented a wholly new challenge for teachers.

At the other end of the spectrum, but often close by, were the predominantly middle class areas, keen to maintain their advantage and pass on their social and cultural capital to their children. Ambitious parents of ambitious children were ready to go to great lengths to ensure their educational success. The two year 6 boys in Bristol described in chapter 1 illustrate the extremes of this spectrum.

The development of the stratification of schools

The developing social and economic spectrum had, as always, its counterpart in the schooling system. Thus the system of schools in the UK after the Second World War was highly stratified. In the top stratum, the traditional public schools, as they are still misnamed, continued to cater for the children of upper class parents as they do now. Just below them was a second tier of independent schools, although this was later to expand. Then came the largely selective schools financed by 'direct grant' from central government, mainly in cities, and then the secondary schools developed and maintained by local education authorities. These were intended to ensure secondary education was universally available, as required by the 1944 Education Act, but these too were stratified, mainly on a bipartite basis (grammar and modern schools), although a tripartite system, to include technical schools, was originally intended (Crook *et al,* 1999).

Grammar schools were intended to cater for only 25 per cent or 30 per cent of children at most (Judge, 1984) and the secondary modern schools began with a predominantly vocational bias (Crook *et al ibid*), approved of by Her Majesty's Inspectors (Judge *ibid*). This corresponded to the world of plentiful work their graduates were expected to enter. In practice, the division between grammar and modern schools was also one of class – the middle classes colonised the grammar schools, particularly after the age of 16, if we take Jackson and Marsden's (1962) account of the situation in Huddersfield as typical, and working class children who did gain entry to them often found it hard to adapt to life there. With the almost linear relationship, at least at first, between attendance at particular schools, qualifications and later occupational status, this was a clear mechanism for the reproduction of class difference.

The development of comprehensive secondary schools with all-ability intakes might have been expected to make this less straight-forward in structural terms and bring about a much wider social mix. There is no doubt that in market towns and rural areas this was so and that comprehensive schools there are a continuing success story, being patronised by parents from a range of social backgrounds (Brighouse, 2002). However, this has not been the outcome in towns and cities.

In London, for example, many former direct grant schools and some voluntary aided grammar schools moved into the independent sector in the 1970s, following the push to comprehensivisation. The heads of the former voluntary aided schools 'reported that the nature of their intake had hardly changed' (Newsam, 1998, p5). The later assisted places scheme, introduced by the conservative government of 1979-83 to provide wider access to private schools, also generally benefited more middle class than working class families. These middle class families were 'high in educational and cultural capital while low in economic capital' (Reay, 2002, p6, quoting Edwards and Whitty, 1997). In this way, class differences continued to be perpetuated in urban areas by school structures of a different sort. Even where there were local area-based comprehensives, they took on the social charac-teristics of the communities they were intended to serve, in practice their class nature. From the 1970s onwards, these schools too became more stratified as a consequence of several related processes.

The stratification was rooted in the fundamental changes taking place in society. For example, people from all social backgrounds became much less willing to accept decisions made about them by others – especially when the people making the decisions would not meet them or were not allowed to do so. The unusual visit to the Education Officer described by Jackson and Marsden (1962) certainly became more usual. These attitude changes are often described as a loss of respect for authority. The greater economic uncertainty experienced by all since the 1970s must have contributed to them, as must the developing values of the consumer society, constantly reinforced by the readily accessible mass media. These changes had a profound influence on schools and not just at the point of choice. They affected people from all classes, even with the widening gap in economic circumstances.

The point is that a much greater proportion of people became more willing to pursue what they wanted and, indeed, believed they should have. For parents, this meant a place at the school they wished their children to attend. The introduction of market forces into the education service from the 1980s onwards, common across the English-speaking world, provided them with the means to accomplish this. Taken together, these changes represented a move from education being seen as a 'citizen right', as Whitty (2002) expresses it, to a 'consumer right', no doubt consistent with the changing values and priorities described.

The mechanisms of the market

So it is hardly surprising that the language used to describe the changing legislation, in the UK at least, also reflected these changing values. The 1992 White Paper *Choice and Diversity: a new framework for schools* (DfE, 1992), already quoted in chapter 2, was a good example, with its clear and useful exposition of the market agenda, ten years into it. It rehearsed the 'themes' of the 1980s, which it considered to have included quality, diversity, parental choice, greater school autonomy and greater accountability. Among the themes it set out for the 1990s, it included successful schools, inspection, the 'demystification of education' (for the consumer) (p7), better testing and more selection. It also expressed its gratification that the 'reality that 'parents know best' has become accepted more and more' (p4).

The market sentiments in this White Paper and its successor, *Self-Government for Schools* (DfEE, 1996) were not notably different from those in *Excellence in Schools* (DfEE, 1997a), published by the Labour government a few weeks after its election. Indeed some of the wording is similar and many of the provisions made by previous conservative governments were left intact by Labour (Whitty, 2002), reflecting consensus on some matters and the irreversibility of others.

The basic market provisions of the legislation in the UK are referred to as *open enrolment*. Parents have the right to express a preference for a particular school. This preference must be acceded to by whichever body is responsible for admitting the children to school (its governing body or local education authority), unless either the school is full (termed 'oversubscribed') or such an admission might conflict with specific aspects of the advertised policy, such as denominational choice or selection on the basis of ability or aptitude. When schools are full, places are allocated on the basis of priorities, which also must have been advertised. These priorities usually include specific medical or special needs which would best be met by going to the school concerned, admission of the younger siblings of children already at the school, and geographical criteria defined by distance or area. There may also be a selection test. Parents have the right to appeal against refusals to offer their children a place and their appeals are considered by panels independent of the admissions body. These panels are empowered to set aside such things as the physical limits of school size, in the interests of allowing a strong and well-based parental preference, on which they adjudicate.

For their part, schools, through the *local management of schools*, are now almost fully autonomous agents in the market. The head and staff are accountable to the governing body for most significant issues, and have complete freedom to act and to spend their budgets within the terms of national frameworks and local education authority policies. Schools receive a budget allocation each year determined by formula. As at least 80 per cent of these budget allocations in each authority's area must be calculated on the basis of pupil numbers at the schools, it is in each school's interests to recruit as many children as possible. The larger the number of children admitted, the larger the budget.

Operating in the quasi-market

Strictly speaking, schooling is not really a market in the pure sense of being a commodity with a price determined by the balance of supply and demand. The reforms which have taken place across the English-speaking world over the past twenty years have merely introduced elements of the market into school provision. Leaving aside what might be called the incidentals of schooling – uniforms, trips and the like, which can nevertheless be expensive – state education is still free at the point of admission. In addition, state schools are not completely autonomous – they are subject to local and national frameworks and are inspected by a public body in England, namely Ofsted. The term 'quasi-market' is therefore often used (see

Whitty *et al*, 1998, p3) and it will be used for the remainder of this book.

As might be expected, the quasi-market is approached in different ways and with different resources by parents, depending on their class background, leading to different outcomes as a consequence. This has been a common theme for some years and Whitty *et al* (1998, p115-122) provide a useful summary of the research data. The differences in resources and outcome are behind the further stratification of schools, particularly at secondary level, which has been taking place since the 1970s.

Not all parents are even likely to be players in the market, as Ball *et al* (1995) say in their London study:

> ..... the former (who engage with the education market) are likely to be middle class, but not all middle class families are strategists and some working class families are. Equally, (those who choose local schools) are typically working class although there are one or two middle class examples. (p411)

So we are talking mainly, but not exclusively, about middle class parents entering the market. How they express a preference is interesting, not just from the point of view of schools which wish to be responsive, but from the point of view of understanding how, in the absence of the previously-colonised grammar schools, they see the most effective ways of passing on their values and priorities to their children – of reproducing themselves.

Expressing a preference

There has been a number of studies of the expression of preference. Ball *et al* (*ibid*) examined the reasons given for choosing schools and types of schools in the early 1990s, in the already highly differentiated school market in London. Reay (2002) considered the attitudes and perceptions of London parents in the allocations process and Bagley *et al* (2001) examined the negative reasoning used by parents (ie for not choosing a school) showing that this completely ruled out the consideration of certain schools. The most detailed recent account of 'class strategies' in this regard is Ball (2003).

In the London context, Reay's qualitative research found that middle class parents often make attributive judgments about institutions – secondary schools and universities – corresponding often to the attributive judgments they make about the young people they assume attend them, for example, from ethnic minorities or the working class. This mirrored Bagley *et al*'s (2001) findings of key reasons for not choosing a school, such as what the pupils at the school were like (judged by appearance or behaviour), school reputation, ethnic composition and also the environment of the school. These show a strong positive preference by these parents for schools which have children 'like us'.

Bristol was one of many local education authorities which undertook its own annual surveys of parents' reasons for choosing particular schools, including those maintained by other authorities and those in the private sector (Bristol LEA, 2000). Overall, these surveys found that 'reputation' and 'results' were the most important factors in determining choice, with reputation largely formed by word of mouth. Advice from primary schools in Bristol had become less important. Like Reay's, the results in Bristol showed that many parents' negative decisions are made without visiting the schools, and on the basis of second or even third hand information – their reputations – something well known to those working in schools. The Bristol parents who were most concerned about academic results in local schools tended to send their children to an independent school and this may have reinforced a class bias.

Schools have always had reputations, of course, but by the early 1990s, these were supplemented and extended by an unprecedented amount of information available to help parental decision making in the quasi-market. Parents can now visit potential schools for their children – and some of them do so more than once (Ball, 2003) – armed with the latest Ofsted inspection report and the annual performance tables. Most of this information is available on the internet, either from home or the local library. It can be supplemented by local knowledge and media reports, many of which too are available online.

Working the system
Working class parents tend not to be market strategists and opt for schools closer to home (Ball *et al*, 1995) because for them getting

the children to school has to be balanced against other family needs such as getting to work. Travel to non-local schools would cost them more. Middle class families by contrast (*ibid*) treat getting the children to the right school every day as the highest priority, presumably because they can afford to do so. Their greater economic capital enables them to express preferences for a wider geographic spread of schools.

Once preferences are expressed, middle class families also bring greater amounts of cultural capital to the admissions process, in terms of their 'knowledge of the system' (Ball *et al*, 1995). This is an advantage because of the complexity of the process, often described as a lottery in the many autumnal media pieces about children who by September have still not found a school place. The process is especially complex when there are large numbers of additional admissions bodies in an area, such as foundation schools, which replaced the former grant maintained schools, or faith schools of the various denominations and religions. If the increasing number of specialist schools were also to select, then this lottery would become even more complicated.

The complexity of the process is compounded by the fact that many of the popular schools favoured by parents are full after more than twenty years of cumulative parental preference. Pupil numbers will certainly have been expanded to their physical limits in these popular schools, and often above them after successful admission appeals.

Gaining access to these popular schools may therefore require the overcoming of several formidable hurdles. For grammar schools and some specialist schools a selection test will need to be passed, using an assessment often based on 'general ability' (Coldron and Williams, 2000). Moving house into a more advantaged area may be necessary so as to meet the geographical criterion (selection by mortgage – Reay, 2002). Or it may just be necessary to play the system skilfully and successfully, expressing simultaneous first preferences through the various admissions procedures, balancing offers of places and making informed appeals.

Middle class families bring greater resources to all of these stratagems: they can bring their knowledge of the system to bear and are more likely to be able to afford to move. In addition, research indicates that their children are more attractive to schools because of the academic success they will bring, and the inexorable connection between results and all 'significant social factors' (Power *et al,* 2002, p13). Their concomitant lower levels of need make fewer demands on the budget, which is really important when places are scarce. Whitty *et al* (1998), quoting earlier research, refer to the offering of places to such children at the expense of others as 'cream-skimming', as these children contribute to the key high stakes numbers in performance tables.

With success comes more success. If the areas around popular schools are largely middle class, they will become more so, favouring more middle class children on the geographical criterion. If admission for older children has been skilfully secured, the younger ones are more likely to be admitted on the sibling rule, and their friends in turn (who are 'like us') will then have a stronger 'wants to move with their friends' case at appeal. All this has the potential to perpetuate the social nature of the intake at these schools which, when judged on the basis of the performance tables, are likely to be higher attaining, cementing school reputations. They will most likely – and certainly more easily – also receive good inspection reports.

The developing stratification

Thus, over a generation, there has been a gravitation towards some secondary schools, for which on a number of counts middle class families have been better placed. What of the schools which are on the other end of this process? The obverse of the positive movement chosen by middle class parents for their children is the negative movement away from the schools held in the poorest regard, as defined by publicly available information and the perceived characteristics referred to by Bagley *et al* (2001). This has meant a movement away from schools with predominantly working class intakes, and some of those with pupils predominantly from ethnic minorities. This has also meant a gravitation away from lower attaining schools, because of the connection between social background and results (Power *et al,* 2002).

At its extreme, the movement begun by middle class parents has been continued by many others, particularly against the backdrop of some of the 'surplus' places in urban areas in the 1980s and 1990s. Solidly working class communities served by some schools, particularly on the blue collar estates, suffered the economic consequences of the recessions of the 1980s and became some of the most disadvantaged communities in the country. The schools left there declined in size, because of demography and the market, and were often left with concentrations of children with very high levels of need, as economic decline was followed by social. They became some of the most challenging schools in which to work, particularly at secondary level; they had never been easy.

Some of these schools suffered a decline in their effectiveness as a consequence. This was not always fully appreciated at the time, as cuts and role changes reduced the presence in schools of local education authority advisers, and Ofsted inspections only commenced in 1993. Some of the schools became difficult to rescue: they often had to admit children excluded from other schools, and their declining size made it more difficult for them to respond adequately to the concentration of need in school and community, despite their generally favourable per pupil funding. There was (and is) the ever-present danger that they could be overwhelmed by their problems and, allied to the problems of turnover, it sometimes became difficult to establish reasonable norms or maintain a sensible perspective, particularly for long-serving staff.

In one such school in Bristol, a new head, who on appointment was well aware of the nature of the school he was taking on, was nonetheless taken aback when confronted in the corridor on his first walk round the school by a group of year 11 students standing chatting, drinking lager and smoking. This was at ten o'clock in the morning; they saw nothing exceptional in what they were doing.

These schools, the victims of political, social and economic history, often became subject to special measures, fresh start or closure. The one in Bristol closed. Many still remain, however, and even if not subject to such a serious decline, they remain vulnerable.

There are similar stories about primary schools, such as the one described in chapter 1, where poverty was being constantly recycled. Families leave as they become better organised or find work, which enables them to move into better housing elsewhere. But they are often only replaced by another disadvantaged family who had reached the bottom of their own particular social trajectory. The age of the children and the size of the school at primary level minimise some of the harshness experienced at secondary level, sometimes reducing the risk. But they too are vulnerable.

The resulting school systems in urban areas

The spectrum of schools which has developed because of the mechanisms of the quasi-market and the uneven outcomes of the pursuit of parental preference has dramatic extremes – the high-attaining secondary school on the one hand favoured by middle class parents and the school on the other which has suffered a dramatic decline in response to that of the communities it serves. The nature of the difference between the extremes, or the extent of the stratification in a school system, will largely depend on the size of the system overall – the numbers of children and the numbers of schools within easy travelling distance – and whether the two social extremes of prosperity and social dissolution exist in large concentrations. In practice, this occurs only in the larger cities. In small market towns and rural areas there may be some stratification at primary level but not at secondary, where there may be only one school. In the larger conurbations, the stratification may go beyond the area covered by one local education authority.

Where the population is served by two or three, or even four or five, secondary schools, stratification will exist between schools – the quasi-market is a national system after all – but it will not be as extreme as that in the major conurbations. Hardship has been experienced in these other communities over the past thirty years – the towns, villages and coastal resorts where traditional industries such as mining, agriculture or fishing may have declined – and will have had its social effects. But the children of more advantaged families will also have to be accommodated in the same smaller school system, ameliorating the effects in the schools in its bottom strata.

Newsam (2002) and Brighouse (2002) have both described seven categories of school in cities resulting from the stratification process, with Brighouse in particular arguing, as has been already noted, that the seven categories can only be fully developed in such areas. They describe 'super-selective' schools, usually in the private sector, and in addition to the formally selective schools in the state sector, the highly desirable schools which take predominantly 'more able' children because of their location, faith requirement, or partially selective nature (as a specialist school). Brighouse talks about the median school as the comprehensive school with a full range of attainment and both say the schools lower down the stratification have progressively fewer children who five years after entry might be expected to achieve the benchmark of five GCSE A*-C grades. Brighouse refers to these schools as 'comprehensive minus', secondary modern and 'secondary modern minus', the latter being at the bottom of the spectrum.

The exact number of categories is not important here, but for schools at the lower end of the spectrum, the declining percentages of children who might be expected to be attaining in the top fifty percent at the age of 16 certainly does. Where the schools are located is also important for school systems. Leaving aside the 'super-selective' schools in the private sector, the highly desirable schools taking large numbers of children likely to be high attainers at 16 and 18 may be situated in the suburbs or more advantaged neighbouring boroughs. As a result, over large sections of major conurbations, the dominant form of secondary school has become those in the lower strata, with some right at the bottom, each with a diminished, and in some cases diminishing, number of children likely to be higher attainers. They will be serving families and communities likely to be predominantly working class, following the flight of middle class families out of them, with more children from ethnic minorities, and some localities of severe disadvantage.

These bottom strata schools are the concern of this book. Providing effectively for the children and young people in them is the fundamental and most important consideration for having good *Schools for Our Cities*. In cities, where there are many bottom strata schools and few or none in the top strata, this is a structural issue as well as one for the functioning of the system as a whole. Newsam (1998) in an earlier article puts it well when he considers:

> ...the ... kind of area ... where school structure is a major problem. These are areas where rich and poor live side by side, where the secondary schools children attend are sharply different in status, in what they achieve and what future they offer to those attending them......

And, he goes on:

> ...the nature and complexity of (these) structural problems appear in their most obvious in urban areas; of which the City of Bristol is not untypical ... just under a quarter of the age group (there attend) independent schools...All the LEA-funded non-selective schools are described as 'comprehensive', reflecting their aspirations rather than the nature of the pupils they admit. (p7)

Bearing in mind who largely benefits from the quasi-market, Newsam notes that '...academically, the continued existence of two nations, particularly in those same urban areas, is starkly obvious' (*ibid*, p5).

This is a phenomenon experienced in many countries (Whitty *et al,* 1998; Kozol, 1991; Anyon and Wilson, 1997; Thrupp, 1999; Thomson, 2002), even though the provisions for parental preference are not as developed elsewhere as they are in the UK. Many of the social and economic changes in these countries – unsurprisingly in the era of a global economy – have been almost exactly the same and have been overlaid by a combination of the policies of the 'new right' (Halsey *et al*, 1997) – education and otherwise – and underpinned by the growing size and aspirations of their middle classes.

The implications of the quasi-market for children

Does any of this matter? Has there not always been a stratified system of schools in the UK? It certainly matters if the quasi-market has led to worse or inadequate provision for some children. There is no doubt that this has been the case for those children left behind in the schools such as the one described in Bristol and this is obviously a good reason for the close attention to school failure considered in chapter 2.

However, some of the changes in schools, as they have strived to maintain or gain market share (Ball, 1994), have clearly been beneficial. Being more responsive to parents is one positive change, as is working to promote orderly behaviour in school and, important for reputation management, to and from school. Other changes, such as those which Whitty *et al* (1998), quoting Gewirtz, characterise as a 'reinvigorated traditionalism' (p89), such as the insistence on uniform or on particular methods of address, may not have harmed children, but may get in the way of preparing children for learning, as discussed in chapter 5. They may take up staff time which could be better spent on learning-related matters. There may also be resistance from some working class children and their parents to these aspects of what Bernstein (1975) terms the *expressive order* of the school, as opposed to the *instrumental order* which encompasses the pursuit of credentials.

The nature of the key indicators required for the performance tables, an important feature of the quasi-market, may also have undesirable effects. They are an issue for all schools in determining their priorities, but for lower attaining ones, they can become top priority, since the indicators are an important element in Ofsted inspection reports and help to determine whether a secondary school is Facing Challenging Circumstances. Drawing on performance data provided by their local education authorities and Ofsted, and using 'additional' or 'catch-up' materials from the national literacy and numeracy strategies, such schools may target the children who might be able to achieve the benchmarks. The needs of other children may therefore become less of a priority, and the narrow concentration on key indicators may further limit schools' capacity to play a wider role in promoting social inclusion (Vincent, 2002). And since the quasi-market in urban areas is more likely to preserve than reduce class differences, as measured by educational mobility, it thus increases social exclusion (Reay, 2002).

Less obvious but nonetheless harmful may be the results of the 'social mix' effect in predominantly working class schools, described by Thrupp (1999) in his study of a system of four schools in New Zealand. Thrupp described what he called a multi-layered effect of different expectations from teachers, more restricted curriculum provision, fewer academic options and enrichments, and lower expectations, both from the children themselves and their parents. This generates a variety of challenges for the teachers related to behaviour, discipline and resistance. Not all Thrupp's findings would necessarily translate to the UK context, particularly since the introduction of the national strategies, but the educational context of bottom strata schools as starting points for learning and effective teaching are the focus of next chapter.

Chapter 4
The context for learning and teaching in bottom strata schools

Setting the context

There are certain significant patterns in UK educational outcomes. We know, for example, that more than twice the proportion (69%) of children of managerial or professional parents (Social Class I and II) achieve five GCSE A*-C grades than those (30%) of unskilled manual parents (Social Class V) (DWP, 2002). We know that 57 per cent of the children of parents who live in owner-occupied homes achieve five A*-Cs compared to 19 per cent of those whose parents live in council-rented property (DWP, 2002).

The Programme for International Student Assessment (PISA) undertaken by the Organisation for Economic Cooperation and Development (OECD, 2001) found that for UK children with parents in the bottom twenty five percent of occupations by status, performance in literacy was more than twice as likely to be in the bottom twenty five percent too. The variations in performance by social class in the UK were similar to those found in the Czech Republic, Hungary and the US and, from a total of 30 countries, were only less extensive than those in Belgium, Germany and Switzerland.

In the bottom strata schools which have emerged in urban areas, there will inevitably be more children from Social Class V (and IV) or with parents in occupations in the bottom twenty five percent by status, than in upper strata schools or in Brighouse's median comprehensives (2002). There will also be a greater proportion of children living in poverty, many of whom will have been included in the above statistics.

The statistics are not in themselves an explanation of the differences in outcomes, but it is nonetheless important to try and provide one if the differences are to be narrowed. This chapter begins by describing in more depth the family and community contexts of bottom strata schools and then considers what happens when they interact with the school's social structure and expectations. Chapters 5 and 6 consider the implications of these interactions for pupils' learning, and then those for teaching and the curriculum.

However, the intractability of the social and economic challenges in many communities served by bottom strata schools requires more than just an educational response, and we return to this later. Meanwhile, three points to note. First, just as each child is different, so is each school. Its unique context for learning and teaching is made up of many individual interactions between school, family and community. The contexts vary from school to school, over time, and in their severity. Second, staff working in a variety of schools will recognise many individual aspects of the day to day school life portrayed in this chapter. In bottom strata schools, however, life is always lived at great intensity, with what might be seen as exceptional in other schools being the norm. Third, because of the quasi-market and the ready availability of the crisis narrative to school observers and stakeholders, it is rare for this virulent and colourful context for learning and teaching to be discussed openly. Within their local markets, many schools would be mortified to see the public appearance of any such accounts.

Poverty and its effects on education

We begin with poverty, because social and material deprivation can significantly damage children's learning.

What is poverty and how extensive is it?

Poverty can be considered in absolute terms, in the sense of a severe deprivation of human needs such as food, health, shelter, drinking water or sanitation, and this sort of poverty can be found in the UK (Howard *et al,* 2001). Usually, however, poverty is taken to be a relative term, signifying a lack of opportunity to participate in, and have access to, what is considered reasonably available in a society. In other words, items from a 'basket of necessities', socially defined, may not be available. Although the deprivation is relative, it is very real to those experiencing it.

Poverty is then measured by the numbers or proportions of people living in households below a certain percentage of median income. Comparisons must be treated with caution, however, especially as different agencies use different criteria for measuring poverty.

Poverty is still significant in the UK. Although a reduction in child poverty is anticipated as the effects of current government policy make themselves felt (Fimister, 2001), income inequality has greatly increased since the late 1960s (Whitty, 2002) and the UK now 'has the highest child poverty rate in the European Union' (Bradshaw, 2002, p17) with 32 per cent of children living in relative poverty (*ibid*). This equates to about four million children under sixteen, many of whom are bound to be attending bottom strata schools.

Poverty can arise in a variety of circumstances through unemployment or low pay, and is most likely to occur in larger families. It is no surprise that lack of work brings a high risk of poverty (77%). So does being a lone parent (61%) (Howard *et al,* 2001). Although the figure has fallen from nearly 19 per cent in the early nineties, 15.5 per cent of children in the UK still live in completely workless households (DWP, 2002). Ethnic minority families are at greater risk of falling into a low-income group or into poverty.

The effects of living in poverty

Living in poverty is intense. It brings a degree of struggle to daily activities such as shopping for food, washing clothes and getting the children to school appropriately dressed and prepared – matters about which many of us don't give a second thought. It can mean going without food in order the feed the children and it can sometimes mean the children going without, leading to short or long term nutritional deficits (Howard *et al,* 2001). It means not being able to visit the supermarket because of the amount of spending required, even though this would be cheaper overall. It can mean living in poor homes, which are possibly damp, and not being able to afford proper heating. It can involve going without household items such as a washing machine or telephone, and not being able to decorate or replace worn out flooring or furniture. It means falling into debt, frequently over everyday expenditure and household items, and sometimes only having access to loans available on the doorstep with punitively high interest rates. It can mean poor health and high mortality rates, and it can mean exclusion from services, ranging from the disconnection of everyday utilities to being unable to go to the pub or cinema. And it can also mean exclusion from social customs (such as Christmas, weddings and funerals), having hobbies or interests, visiting friends or relations or having them round for a meal (all from Howard *et al,* 2001).

The personal effects of living in poverty are reported to include always being tired and feelings of isolation and rejection. People often feel stigmatised and there is a greater incidence of mental health problems (Howard *et al,* 2001). Crime is a constant worry, especially in many communities in which poor people live.

For children and young people, poverty means being unable to participate in the lifestyles of many of their peers. They may have to go without toys, books, or a second-hand bicycle and not have a separate bedroom when they get older. A large proportion of children may fail to reach recommended nutrient levels and those in Social Class V are more likely by the age of fifteen to report long-standing illness. They can be smaller (2.25 centimetres at the age of five in deprived areas) and perform poorly in cognitive development tests, on average 3.7 percent behind the children who come from homes with incomes in the top fifth. Even by the age of 22 months, children from Social Classes IV and V can be 14 percentage points behind children in Social Classes I and II in educational development. Fifty thousand children in the UK are 'heavily involved' in caring for a family member who is chronically ill or disabled, which puts the family into another high risk group for living in poverty (Howard *et al,* 2001 and Bradshaw, 2002).

Parents living in poverty speak for themselves
Research studies which interviewed people living in poverty about how they manage and how they see their situation paint a vivid picture and Howard *et al* (2001) and Bradshaw (2002) draw on these in their summaries. One report from a voluntary organisation based on

interviews with 122 individuals from 39 families (ATD Fourth World, 2000) draws out the implications for education. Although only a small survey, it provides some practical insight into some of the effects of living in poverty.

The survey found the parents interviewed to be aspirant, in the sense that they hoped that education would 'provide their children with the chances they never had' (p6) and that they were well-informed. Nevertheless, only six of the 39 families interviewed had what they described as a 'good relationship' with their children's schools, although this finding is not easy to interpret. In these six cases, at least, the parents felt they were treated as full partners and that bullying, for example, which features extensively in the report, was dealt with well by the school.

Many of the interviewees suffered from the low levels of self-efficacy described by Whitty (2002) – an inability, real and perceived, to influence the things which adversely affect one's life. Some, for example, did not know how to ask for extra help for their children and at secondary school in particular, to whom to speak. Some perceived their own limited education (for a variety of reported reasons) as a problem in helping their children. Others found it difficult when 'negative views' were expressed to them by schools about their children, often when they had been in trouble. One parent found it difficult to agree to get her child on time to school because, as she put it, she didn't know what might be happening the next day. As a consequence, some parents described meetings at school where they were 'swearing' or 'screaming and shouting' (p21) because of their own frustration. It is easy to see how these families could become pathologised by the school and labelled as 'problem families' (Howard *et al,* 2001).

Bullying was mentioned by thirty out of thirty nine families interviewed, presumably rather more than would be found in a more socially representative cross-section. When not dealt with adequately (the majority of the cases according to the families), the reported legacy was unhappy children. They were reluctant to go to school, or missed schooling while they were in the process of being moved by their parents to another one. In some cases, it was reported by the families that children had reacted violently to being bullied and this partly explains why a fifth of the families had also experienced the exclusion of one or more of their children.

Missing school for such reasons or due to poor health or moving home was mentioned many times by the people interviewed. When added to the difficulties of meeting the costs of the correct uniform and school trips, having access to the appropriate equipment such as calculators or computers and dealing with the trauma suffered by some of the children because of their violent childhoods, a compelling picture emerges of the difficulty that many of these children and their parents find in participating fully in their school communities and activities. As the authors of the report say:

> There are a host of other issues (besides lack of money) which people living in poverty have to contend with. Many of these impact directly on the children's ability to benefit from education...... Poverty should not be an excuse for poor educational achievement, but it can be an explanation. (*ibid*, p47)

The effects on children's schooling

Children living in poverty may have interrupted schooling, may find it less easy to concentrate through tiredness or malnutrition, may be involved in bullying and may sometimes be stigmatised by their peers. They may not have the basics for school such as appropriate dress or equipment, even when their teachers are understanding and try to provide them with support. They may not be able to go on school visits and trips. At home, they will not have the cultural artefacts, such as books or computers, possessed by their peers in more affluent homes. They may not have the opportunity to visit a library and will not be taken to the theatre or cinema by their parents. They will not receive as much assistance at home and may not themselves feel self-confident or in control. They will begin school, and may continue there, having possibly had less intellectual stimulation than children in other social classes. When in school, they may often have other things on their mind even when their parents have explained the importance of schooling for their future lives.

Like their parents, 'children will be vulnerable to low levels of self-efficacy' (Whitty, 2002, p113). They too may feel apprehension, apathy or despair and may be less likely to accept and be enthusiastic about the challenges of school. If learning and its routines, rituals and symbols seem completely alien to their experiences with peer group, family and community, their apprehension, apathy or despair will be further compounded. This is the experience of the year 6 boy in the Bristol special school described in chapter 1. And for children of families experiencing temporary homelessness, they may not even be able to get to school without assistance (Clark, 1993; ATD Fourth World, 2000) or have to change schools.

The connections between occupational group and literacy (OECD, 2001) and between social class and GCSE (DWP, 2002; Power *et al,* 2002) have been noted. And children who truant are more likely to have parents from poorer backgrounds, who are in low-skilled rather than managerial jobs, and who live in local authority housing (Social Exclusion Unit, 1997). We know that children who are excluded are more likely to come from broken families and poorer backgrounds. These children will probably, though not exclusively, be attending schools serving communities with high levels of disadvantage (Social Exclusion Unit, 1997; Pearce and Hillman, 1998), which includes bottom strata schools.

It is surely right that national policy attends to the circumstances which give rise to poverty, but it needs to be noted that the effects of living in poverty are likely to continue in terms of general self-efficacy, even when families have been lifted out of low income brackets (Howard *et al,* 2001). As Coles and Kenwright (2002) say:

> ... the effect of deprivation seems to have a long term effect... while individuals and families may move in and out of social disadvantage, the association between deprivation and educational attainment in primary school is likely to persist throughout an individual's career (p248)

Even with a twenty year timetable beginning in 1999 to end child poverty (Fimister, 2001), some of the social effects will linger in school and in society for some time after that. It is a long term problem.

There are also children who attend bottom strata schools who come from families which have never fallen within the official definitions of poverty, but who nonetheless share some of these social characteristics. Many more children than the 32 per cent identified in the UK as living in poverty will bring some aspects of the disadvantages described into school.

The learning and teaching context for bottom strata schools

Children's attitudes to school affect how they learn and approach school life in general. And the cultural settings in which children learn at home and in the community may differ in important respects from those predominating at school.

Attitudes to school

Children's attitudes to school are shaped by many factors, including the experiences and expectations of family and community and their own interests. As they grow older, do they consider school relevant to what they might want to do when they leave? Do they feel the personal demands school makes on them are acceptable or in conflict with the things they would rather be doing?

Blatchford's (1996) study in 'inner city, largely working class areas' gives us some insight into the attitudes of children and young people attending bottom strata schools. He found that older children lost interest in school, with 26 per cent of 16 year olds finding school mostly interesting, 53 per cent 'mostly in the middle', 16 per cent mostly boring and 5 per cent 'other'. Black children tended to find school more interesting than white and the children who did find school interesting tended to be attaining more highly. But 41 per cent of 16 year olds felt negative about going to school in the morning, although this seems related to having to get there each day rather than to just what it was like. The good thing about school they most often cited was 'seeing friends and having fun with them' (41%), although lessons and work also feature in both the best and the worst things and 93 per cent of the young people thought school important for getting a good job.

Staff in many schools will recognise these attitudes in the young people they teach. Although attendance at school is considered important and most find some of it interesting, there are many parallel experiences considered more engaging. This means that school rituals and symbols are likely to be tolerated, but challenged at the margins in relation perhaps to such things as dress and jewellery. Aspects of the day-to-day running of the school such as notions of acceptable behaviour and punishment will also have negotiable elements.

Many young people who do not consider school important will be on the way to becoming casualties by the age of 16. The Social Exclusion Unit's (1999) report *Bridging the Gap* found that nationally nearly 10 per cent of the 16-18 year group were not in education, employment or training and the figure was higher in urban areas. As the report comments:

> 16 is a critical point when for some, problems that have been brewing for years reach a crisis, and for others, problems begin that could have been avoided. Both groups – and society more generally – bear the costs for years to come. (p8)

For many of these young people, education has lost its point and there is a risk that the cycle of poverty and low pay will be continued into another generation. Some will have decided not to make the effort at school after experiencing difficulties or persistent failure and many will have found little encouragement at home to persevere. Others will have been seduced by alternatives available from quite an early age such as low-paid, unskilled or illegal work. Some may have found the tangible symbols of status offered by the illegal drugs industry – money, power over others, clothes and later cars – irresistible for what appears to be less hard work and sacrifice. The prospect of an early and glamorous, albeit dangerous, fast track into adulthood will have won out against the extended childhood of school. This continues to be a serious matter. In the UK, 2003 began as two teenage girls were killed on New Year's Eve in a hail of bullets from the cross fire between two street gangs, precipitating national concern about the prevalence of guns in cities.

Learning in home and community

When they start school, children may be emergent bilinguals speaking a variety of European, Asian or African languages, and first learning to express themselves in English (Gregory, 1997). They will then grow and live with more than one language, each with its differing cultural assumptions built into its grammar and syntax.

Children may be growing up with a variety of oral traditions at home and in the community, for example of story-telling. There may be different ways of conversing with adults: they may be used to being addressed rather than spoken with; they may not be expected to respond to the attention of adults but show a respectful silence, and there may be nuances according to generation, gender or status.

The children may have begun to learn in organised groups when they were very young and may continue to do so as they get older. They may be studying the Qur'an or sacred texts of other religions, including Christianity, and learning Arabic or other additional languages not spoken at home. They may be learning in large classes and very formal teaching settings. At home, the children may have responsibilities in the household which increase with age and vary with gender.

Children move between quite different contexts, therefore, and sometimes between several (Wrigley, 2000). While some will do so successfully, being able to bring their accomplishments from one setting to another, others will find it difficult and bewildering. As they get older, the different contexts and values implicit in them will mix and cross-fertilise constantly in their minds with the values of the consumer society in which they are growing up, building identities that are distinct from those of their elders.

Barriers to classroom learning and teaching

This complexity in the home and community backgrounds of young people attending bottom strata schools brings a rich diversity to their classroom learning. Without doubt, some of this can be positive, if received appropriately, but much will clearly be negative, erecting potential barriers to learning which require measured and thoughtful responses from teachers. This is not always easy and the nature of these potential barriers to learning and teaching are now explored, as they set the context for the work of the staff with which this chapter concludes. The origins of many of these barriers to learning and teaching are similar but, although related, they present differently in the school context, requiring different responses.

Lack of communication

Lack of communication, or at least purposeful communication, between adults and young people is the first barrier. Sometimes this is put down as an inability to communicate on the part of working class children and they are said to lack 'communicative language'. It was reported in the early 1990s, for example, that a third of the children in the reception class of a school serving an estate in Bristol had 'no language at all' and could not communicate anything.

But working class children do have a rich linguistic context at home, as established in a comparative study decades ago by Tizard and Hughes (1984). This has been confirmed since – by Tizard *et al* (1988) and by Brooker (2002), who undertook an ethnographic study of Anglo and Bangladeshi children and their families attending a particular primary school. The problem as she expresses it is that these studies had:

> ... not entirely eliminated a persistent earlier supposition that children from lower social groups 'lack language'. Children from different social groups, as we have known since the early work of Basil Bernstein, may talk in different ways, but they have the whole range of communicative skills available to them within their habitual speech repertoire. Whether teachers (who themselves very often originate from different social and cultural groups from the children's) can respond to the children's home language patterns is another matter entirely. (*ibid*, p9/10)

The lack of communicative language is imputed not just to children for whom English is an additional language, but African Caribbean, white working class and other children. The research tells us that this is a matter of linguistic convention in the classroom, or the use of different language patterns from those in use at home, as she says.

In illustration of this, Tizard and Hughes (*ibid*) had identified certain conversational habits of nursery staff with children, centred on the questioning techniques considered appropriate at the time, which they felt were disadvantageous to working class children. In a different context, when African American children are asked obvious-answer questions in class, common in middle class homes (are you doing a drawing for me?), they can be perplexed as they never have conversations of this kind with adults at home or in the community (NRC, 2000).

If the problem is identified as the children's, inaccurate assumptions may be made about their potential, based on their apparent inability to conform to classroom expectations. The real barrier to their learning – or at least the first which must be considered when children do not respond – is the fact that the linguistic conventions of the classroom privilege the communications of some children over others.

A barrier of a contrary nature may arise when the students themselves use the linguistic conventions of peer or street culture to exclude staff – and some of their peers – deliberately and to embody their resistance to school expectations and culture (Mac an Ghaill, 1988). These are considered later.

Social needs

Much has been said about social needs – hunger, worry, poor health, or the sorts of problem experienced by the Year 6 special school boy referred to in chapter 1. And there are the personal challenges faced by children in public care, who may have experienced neglect or abuse, and for whom learning may be the last thing on their minds when they arrive at school. And even when they are eager to learn, the vividness of the other parts of their lives may keep intruding, erecting mental barriers to their learning.

Low expectations

Teachers' low expectations of pupils have long been held to contribute to their poor achievement in urban schools and hence be a barrier to children's learning. This was an important conclusion of the HMI survey of urban education in the 1990s (Ofsted, 1993). Teachers' assumptions that children lack language, when in reality they are reflecting their perplexity at the classroom environment, is one way that low expectations arise. Another is when teachers make attributive judgements about children, based on what they think they are like, as revealed in the Gillborn and Youdell (2000) study. Such judgments are much like those made by some of the parents described in the last chapter.

Any such negative assumption communicates itself to the children and may be compounded by the expectations of parents and of the children themselves. Parents who themselves have had little educational success or have found school a difficult experience, will either not have, or be wary of having, high expectations of their own children's achievement (Dyson and Robson, 1999).

Without the cultural experience of educational success, it is difficult to imagine what it might be like or what its practical implications might be from day to day. When children experience difficulty learning or making progress, such parents find it hard to provide support or encouragement at home, and the children themselves may not understand clearly what educational success could be like for them. The low or negative expectations of their parents and teachers become the dominant and limiting picture of their potential in their own minds.

Poor motivation and self-confidence

The lack of motivation and self-confidence arising from such circumstances will reduce the effort young people expend on their learning and endanger their potential achievement. A survey in the US found that two thirds of teenagers 'readily admitted they could do much better in school if they tried' and reported an unsurprising connection between the long term engagement with learning and school achievement (NRC, 1999, p30).

The danger is that lack of motivation or self-confidence might lead to a much stronger alienation from school, reflecting a wider alienation in their lives. Bruner (1996) eloquently discussed the alienation of some of the young in the US, as they considered the 'staggering lopsided distribution of wealth and earnings' and the inequalities in outcomes for them. He went on to say:

> Kids may not know the figures, but they also sense it in the air, as on the 'real' agenda......

> But for reasons of delicacy, perhaps, or expediency, this is a topic that gets left out of school. Enough such leavings out, and school begins to present so alien or so remote a vision of the world that many learners can find no place in it for them or their friends. This is true not just of girls, or blacks, or Latinos, or Asians, or other kids we target for special attention as potentially at risk. There are also those restless, bored kids in our sprawling suburbs who suffer the pandemic syndrome of 'What am I doing here anyway? What's this got to do with me?' (p97/8)

This goes far beyond bottom strata schools. The alienation of middle class boys is becoming a concern for the education service in the UK and is beyond the scope of this book. But the apathy and helplessness with which many young people in bottom strata schools regard their situation and their burning sense of injustice can be very strong, as shown by Kozol (1995) in his account of the reactions to poverty and the prospects for children growing up in the South Bronx.

The sense of injustice about the 'otherness' of school culture which, as Bruner says, young people may feel reflects what they perceive to be wrong in the wider society, such as its failure to acknowledge the presence or history of black Britons, feeds into peer and street cultures, which are often anti-learning.

Alienated from society or not, all young people may at times be distracted by the trappings, gadgets and values of peer culture, such as the importance of friendship groups, an emphasis on relationships, or the urgency of communication engendered by mobile phones. The successors to the young people who were the subject of Blatchford's (1996) study would expect to take these things in their stride – plus clubbing and many hours on computer games – alongside their attendance at school.

Lack of self-confidence may be endemic in children with little family history of educational success, but it may also arise from low expectations and persistent failure at school. Children may develop coping or avoidance strategies as a result, which for some will carry over into adulthood, making it harder to support them educationally. It is important this barrier is recognised early and receives a response. Barber (1996a) describes how doing nothing may lead to young people first being disappointed, then becoming disaffected and later, possibly, among the 'disappeared'.

School resistance

School resistance is one of the coping or avoidance strategies adopted by pupils as a way of maintaining self-respect while avoiding learning. It is often a strong expression of alienation from the authority and world of the school. It can be made on class grounds – the strong tradition of school resistance in white working class communities (Jackson and Marsden, 1962) continues unabated in some today – but also on racial or religious grounds.

School resistance among some ethnic minority groups – African Caribbean and Asian adolescents, for example – may be articulated in terms of perceptions of the racist nature of school and society, but may also be an expression of masculinity (Mac an Ghaill, 1988, Sewell, 1997). The studies of these dynamics, the descriptions of the schools concerned, and the behaviour of some staff, all show how such positioning can be compounded and impede learning. The boys' resistance could be seen as a response to barriers sometimes erected by staff. Even teachers not culpable of overt discrimination can be seen as complicit when they support unjust punishment or discipline.

A range of stances can be taken by young men and women. At one extreme, resistance can manifest itself as disobedience and refusal to accept school norms, for example, by not taking examinations seriously and refusing to respect the discipline of the examination hall. Or resistance can appear as a quieter but more determined acquiescence, self-explained as not giving excuses for punishment or discrimination and getting what is possible out of the system.

Mac an Ghaill (1988) included a group of young African Caribbean women as part of his study. Whilst accepting the realities of the world and school as seen by their male counterparts, these young women had decided to deal with the racialised education system on its own terms and were at sixth form college preparing to apply to university. They had made a conscious decision to learn and over-come the barriers to learning, including those they could have erected for themselves. They would not accept, however, the expressive order of the institutions they attended. How this affects the overall milieu of the school or that of individual classrooms depends on whether a critical mass is achieved.

Other aspects of cultural dissonance

There may be other aspects of conflict and resistance in school which will affect what students are able to achieve. All children from another class or ethnicity than their teachers, or who do not share their cultural assumptions, will feel torn at some time during their educational careers, particularly if they have particular personal goals in mind – for example, a teenager from a Pakistani family who feels bombarded by the values of the consumer society, which infuse the interests and narratives of his peers from all communities. He might wish to retain his respectful loyalties to his own family and community – without agreeing with absolutely everything they stand for or behaving in the ways they do – and to speak and under-stand Urdu. He may have been taken 'back' to Pakistan by his parents. He feels some of what the Asian youths in Mac an Ghaill's (*ibid*) study feel about their school, but wishes to get on. This is a constant background in this young person's mind as he comes to school each day and tries to engage with the learning experiences his teachers have prepared for him. Even with motivation and self-confidence, these other conflicts could distract him from learning and form a mental barrier he has to overcome.

Attendance and turnover

Pupil attendance at school is generally lower in bottom strata schools and the level of pupil turnover can be significant in some of them. If children do not attend school, they cannot learn, and if their schooling is discontinuous and they are repeatedly faced with having to make new relationships with peers and teachers, their learning will suffer. Lack of continuity in classes makes it difficult for teachers to maintain continuity of expectation and support children adequately, particularly if they are traumatised.

Even in schools achieving the national benchmarks for measuring school attendance (90 per cent for secondary and 92 per cent for primary schools), some children will miss much of their schooling. A few children attend for less than half the time, a larger group attend slightly more often and so on. These pupils have already become the disappeared, but feature in the school's data in the performance tables. Many bottom strata secondary schools fail to achieve the 90 per cent benchmark and attendance deteriorates progressively through the year groups, approaching 70 per cent or worse by year 11.

Pupil turnover is high in bottom strata schools serving large refugee communities, where children can arrive and disappear quickly; in those serving communities with large housing turnover such as in the junior school in chapter 1; and in schools on local authority housing estates which are being refurbished, with families being moved out by the council, sometimes at short notice.

Behaviour

The negotiated nature of classrooms in bottom strata schools, where authority is likely to be challenged more often, affects the incidence of behaviour perceived as unacceptable. Such behaviour has become a significant matter for teachers – 45.1 per cent of secondary teachers leaving the profession prematurely gave pupil behaviour as a reason in 2001, just behind workload at 57.8 per cent (Smithers and Robinson, 2001). They and parents see it as a major impediment to the learning of all the children in the classes affected; perceptions of it are important in the quasi-market (Bristol LEA, 2000).

There is a delicate line to be negotiated by teachers in situations of conflict with young people where staff authority and professional expertise might be seen to be undermined and the learning of other children disrupted in the interests of including a challenging young person in a class or school. Staff expect to be supported by school leadership teams if conflict arises or an excluded child is returned to school following appeal. Conflict can arise. For example, in one school in Bristol, a year 8 girl called her young teacher by an unpleasant sexually-loaded name, pushed her over and threatened her with violence in the community as she ran out of the door. The girl received a fixed term exclusion of two days.

This is serious behaviour, whatever gave rise to it, and can be compounded from the school's point of view by a family's apparent unwillingness to work with staff or their perceived abusive behaviour towards them. This is the staff perception of the distressing meetings reported by parents in the ATD Fourth World study (2000). One boy of reception age in Bristol, for example, continually assaulted children in his class, it was alleged, spoke to girls in a sexualised manner and kicked members of staff who tried to restrain him, including his headteacher. His mother and grandmother did not accept the school's accounts of his behaviour and came to school every day, sitting in the reception area until they were spoken to. This often took a great deal of time. The boy eventually went to a residential school, although it was some time before his mother would permit her son to be assessed formally. The pressures of dealing with such a demanding family in a relatively small school led to staff falling ill or losing confidence, and this undoubtedly contributed to the school's being judged by Ofsted to require special measures.

An extreme case such as this often occurs against a background of more general disruption in classrooms. Even at primary level, this calls for special skills from the staff and can change the environment for the learning of all children. The head of one large primary school in Bristol serving a white working class area often said that teachers had to be good in her school to be considered satisfactory by Ofsted, and excellent to be considered good – general sentiments echoed by Her Majesty's Chief Inspector of Schools (Ofsted, 2003). When a teacher was away from school, she explained, her children would 'go wild'. This has many implications for the day to day leadership and management of urban schools, and for the recruitment of effective supply teachers, if classrooms are to remain calm.

Educational needs

The interplay between social, physical and learning needs is a complex one, but one of the consequences is that bottom strata schools also have a higher proportion of children with assessed special educational needs than those serving more advantaged areas. These children will need extra support and attention if they are to learn, requiring resources identified by the school or provided by the local education authority. There will be more such children in classrooms and the school is likely to have to make its own specialist provision for them.

Working with parents and the community

Schools' work with parents and the community, if successful, will positively reinforce learning and minimise time-consuming negative conflict with families.

The research on both the problems and successful practice is thin, often arising from small-scale projects deemed to be successful by their originators. In many of the communities served by bottom strata schools, it is the 'silent group' of parents who may be causing concern and about whom the staff need to know more (Dyson and Robson, 1999) so that the specific presenting problems of their children can be responded to appropriately.

A secondary headteacher in Bristol used to speak of 'the hopelessness at the school gate' to describe how difficult his school found it to engage parents. His words reflect the lack of self-efficacy discussed earlier and the end of community in some areas. A local politician described how, when canvassing on a local authority housing estate, an aging constituent described how she had watched one of her neighbours burgle another in broad daylight. She was too frightened to call the police herself and, in any case, she did not think they would come. Another man had his artificial pond stolen one night. The next day, one exactly like it appeared fully installed in his neighbour's garden, who maintained he had acquired it cheaply elsewhere.

These circumstances make the task of the school more difficult:

> Insofar as the literature deals in any detail with community and family diversity, its principal concern is the way in which some communities and families experience a greater distance between themselves and the schools which their children attend than do others. The implication is that where there are significant ethnic, cultural and social divides between schools, families and communities, schools and their partners..... have to work that much harder to bridge those divides. (Dyson and Robson, 1999, p28)

Not only do the schools have to work harder to bridge this divide, as Dyson and Robson say, they also have to sustain their efforts (Mortimore and Whitty, 2000). The potential divide between parents and school does not mean, however, that working class parents are less engaged with their children than middle class parents. The evidence shows the contrary (Tizard and Hughes, 1984; Ball *et al,* 1995; ATD Fourth World, 2000; Reay, 2002), but parents may feel marginalised by staff, even with the variety of initiatives now available nationally, because of the staff's 'cultural imperialism' (Dyson and Robson, 1999) and their apparent assumptions of superiority. Parents from some cultural backgrounds may be 'invisible' (Brooker, 2002) even when they are anxious to be involved, because of a barrier erected by the staff.

Contacts do take place between parents and staff in bottom strata schools but they may be brief and intense. Direct challenges might be made to headteachers in the playgrounds, for example, often with another adult and child present, by parents unhappy with the way some matter concerning their children has been dealt with. These challenges will be conducted just as they might be at home and soon forgotten.

Headship in such communities can be extremely demanding. It may begin with what might be termed a negative honeymoon period until acceptance is gained and the community decides 'you are all right'. Or not – when the situation can quickly become untenable.

What it is like for the staff

This context for learning and teaching in bottom strata schools presents staff with a variety of additional pressures in carrying out their routine professional duties. Teachers have to spend much time on matters apparently incidental to learning but without which there would be a dramatic reduction in purposeful work in classrooms. Children generate huge personal demands, arising from their insecurity, poor self-organisation, not having the appropriate dress or materials, and their lack of confidence, perhaps because of what is going on at home or in the community. Staff have to deal with lateness, or non-attendance, often for understandable reasons, every day. They have to negotiate many aspects of their routine expectations of the pupils, some of whom may wish to challenge them, and they cannot assume automatic obedience. They will often feel drained.

Relationships across the school may be fragile at times or between certain groups of children. Relationships may be dramatically affected by large or small community events, or even the ripples of interpersonal ones. Racial conflict may be an issue in the school or community or both.

Staff need to provide special support and assistance to young people at all such times; when things blow up in classrooms, extra assistance will be needed there. Vigilance and attention to the emotional atmosphere of the school is necessary to ensure it remains calm, anticipate disturbances and establish and maintain a working atmosphere. In secondary schools, staff face the risk daily of incidents or disorder arising from the large scale movement round the site. This is less severe in the primary school, leaving intruders aside, but there too children may fall out badly, reflecting and carrying community conflict into the playground or classroom. Teachers must be alert to such situations, and have the skills to deal with them.

Many children will be involved with professionals outside school, including psychologists, youth workers, educational welfare officers, social workers or the police. The intractability of some of their problems involves referral of more of them to such agencies, especially since it is only in school that they are regularly seen and a wider picture of their needs constructed. This requires the staff to have sufficient time to be able to do this adequately.

Many children may have behaviour as well as learning needs. At primary school, there may also be physical or toileting needs. At secondary, the presenting needs may be compounded if the school has admitted children excluded from other schools.

As Pat Thomson (2002) says about provision at 'disadvantaged schools':

> ...Teachers contend daily with myriad contextually produced mundane and routine frustrations, achievements, sadnesses and micro-politics, and struggle to find the words to explain how it is that relentlessly focusing on learning is easier to say than do. (p17)

When it comes to teaching, staff may find their usual repertoire of skills does not work (Thrupp, 1999) and, to try and ensure effective learning is taking place, may have to modify them. They may need to organise and pace their lessons differently and abandon adventurous approaches. They will be confronted more often and the negotiated nature of the classroom, particularly as the pupils get older, may mean they restrict what they offer (Hallinger and Murphy, 1986; Thrupp, 1997). Beginnings and endings of lessons may be ragged and take up time, reducing the core learning time. Teachers will have to do more catching up, partly because of poor attendance, and may have to provide more small-step scaffolding for learning and give children constant re-assurance. Relations with parents (and siblings and other relatives) may be intense or problematic and may sometimes erupt into school, requiring staff vigilance and the availability of immediate assistance.

And at the same time, staff in bottom strata schools, particularly at secondary level, are operating within the quasi-market. They must maintain the confidence of parents who, if they are unhappy and there are places at other schools, could take their children away, putting additional pressure on the school budget and what the school is able to do. And parental unhappiness can be exacerbated by negative media coverage, community issues and local conflicts.

This is the presenting context for learning and teaching in bottom strata schools. The schools have a 'relentlessness' about them, even when things seem to be going well. It never stops. There is the ever-present possibility of things going wrong, affecting staff and parental confidence. No school may be able to stand still, in terms of improving or getting worse (Stoll and Fink, 1995), but the combination of what has been described in this chapter and the last suggests that bottom strata schools are also potentially the most unstable. The cumulative effect of what might individually be considered small events can build up quickly. These schools can move very quickly from one category of organisational health to another. Schools perceived as successful and functioning well one year may not be so the next.

Chapter 5
Learning in bottom strata schools

Bringing children to learning

The picture of bottom strata schools painted in the last chapter reveals the reality of instability and potential risk. In the worst scenario, where the potential of all the risks is realised at once – communication failure, widespread defiance of authority, poor behaviour and hostile parent groups – the school can be overwhelmed. More usually, schools realise how close they are coming to this sort of crisis and take appropriate action. This requires the vigilance described in the last chapter, but also unrelenting hard work (Mortimore and Whitty, 2000). It demands sustained effort.

Having to work harder than in more advantaged areas will attract only the most dedicated staff. Extra resources help, but they do not change the daunting nature of the task in bottom strata schools as it is currently framed. In this chapter and the next, it is argued that the work of these schools needs to be firmly based on an understanding of the nature of learning and the ways that children's personal histories, preferences and learning in other contexts influence their learning in school. So although all state schools need to be ambitious for their children and introduce them to the international canon, they need to design their teaching and curricular programmes around their pupils.

Children's minds are not, as was once thought, *tabula rasa* on which the teacher, adult or world may write, irrespective of who the children are. Learning is a dynamic process of interplay between children and their environment which changes the structures of their brains (NRC, 2000; Claxton, 1999). If staff understand this dynamic process, they can draw children into learning from their own starting points, being clear about what they can learn, how and when, and how learning in school and other settings can be mutually reinforcing. This then is a sound basis for effective teaching and curricular programmes in all schools, but essential in bottom strata schools.

Many children begin in bottom strata schools in the UK with disadvantages which continue throughout their educational careers. By the time they take national examinations at the age of 16, the gap between their measures of attainment and those of more advantaged young people has widened considerably (Gillborn and Mirza, 2000). These widening differences alone should be enough to persuade teachers and policy makers that what we are doing at the moment is inadequate. The primacy of these children's disadvantages outside school directly affects their lack of success within it. If the socially-based gap in outcomes in the UK is to be narrowed, some attempt must also be made to reproduce for the children in bottom strata schools the learning advantages of their more fortunate peers.

Learning as a social process

How children's disadvantages outside school determine their learning is explored using a theoretical model of what they bring to the learning process, wrapped up in who they are. The model was developed after an extended ethnographic study of children's learning at primary school (Pollard with Filer, 1996) which related the influence of factors in children's backgrounds and histories to how they approached and benefited from school. The model has been further developed in Broadfoot *et al* (2000) and Pollard and Triggs (2000). It explains the complexities and components of learning through a model of learning as a *social process*, as illustrated in Figure 1.

The model also shows learning as a cyclical process, beginning and ending with the individual learner, developing and changing through the cycle. Initially, children develop views about themselves – what they are like, what they can do and how they should behave – as their relationships with family, peers and teachers unfold. This is their identity, which then determines how they bring their *potential* and their *resources* into the learning process itself.

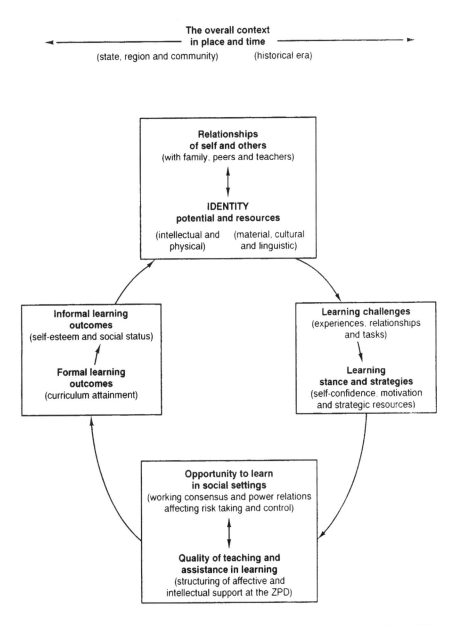

Figure 1:A Social Model of Learning (taken from Pollard with Filer (1996) p97)

Their *potential* can be intellectual or physical and is not assumed to be a given. It is the outcome of previous learning and development, and the complex interplay between genetic inheritance and environment. It is also the capacity that children bring to the next stage of the learning process.

Their *resources* are material, cultural or linguistic. Material resources are the nature and quality of their home, the books and toys they have had access to, and the other experiences they have such as holidays or regular swimming in a local pool. Cultural resources are what they have accumulated from their various relationships, such as how they behave towards other people, their understanding of the meaning and significance of different occasions (including going to school), their personal application to tasks, and the confidence they might have developed as a consequence. Linguistic resources include the ability to speak and understand a language, the ability to relate to the dominant language patterns and conventions in different settings, and the ability to use language to support their own thinking and learning.

With their potential and their resources, children approach learning challenges (right hand box of Figure 1). These arise from experiences when new things are encountered, when they visit new places, and through their relationships with parents, relatives and others. Challenges arise from tasks they have been set in school or have set themselves, which require conscious or unconscious thought to complete, or which have unexpected elements to them.

Drawing on their *potential* and their *resources*, children approach these learning challenges with a *learning stance* and with their *strategies*. These are their level of *motivation*, their *self-confidence* and their *strategic resources*. Their motivation and self-confidence are particularly related to the nature of the learning required – whether it is clear or ambiguous, it requires learners to try something new, and whether they feel it is something they can accomplish because they have done something like it before. Their strategic resources are the *resources for learning* they have accumulated and can bring to bear. Do they have techniques for approaching particular mathematical puzzles or the chess game they have been asked to play? Do they have mental strategies for tackling tasks such as writing to their aunt in America? Do they have general strategies for their learning and reflection? Do they know how to start the learning task and can tell when they have finished? Can they keep themselves on task even when they get frustrated?

How children approach learning challenges in general – their stance and their strategies – will determine how they benefit from *opportunities to learn in social settings*, the bottom box of Figure 1, representing learning in classrooms. In these social settings, there will be further more complex relationships, but also the positive possibility of enhanced learning through teaching and further conscious assistance.

Finally, the learning cycle has both formal and informal outcomes. The formal outcomes will ideally be achievement of the desired learning objectives for the lesson, including specific subject-related performance outcomes related to the structure of the national curriculum. They could also include further *strategic resources* for learning as described. There are also informal outcomes: self-esteem is enhanced by mastering something new or understanding a new concept, and this might enhance self-confidence next time. And there may be a gain in social status, affecting how significant others, such as their teachers, or parents, peers and friends, perceive and behave towards the child.

Positive formal and informal outcomes increase children's potential and resources and their capacity for further learning. This carries over into the learning stance and strategies they bring to the next learning challenge – and so it goes on. At each stage of the cycle, there are factors which could strengthen it – push it further on its way and increase potential learning – or weaken it and decrease the potential learning. The more positive each stage of the cycle, the stronger the next one will be. This is how the cumulative steps or gaps between learning outcomes for children develop over time and how the material, social and other disadvantages experienced by many children in bottom strata schools become learning disadvantages.

How learning disadvantage arises

Consider identity first – the top box of Figure 1 (p63). The richer the complex interplay of relationships and the more opportunities children have to learn from challenges or in social settings, the more they will develop their intellectual and physical potential, and the more they will accumulate material, cultural and linguistic resources to bring to further learning. This is true at all stages of their lives.

Children living in poverty are likely to have less physical potential than their more advantaged peers because of their diet and consequent size. Children with poor access to learning challenges and opportunities before they start school, and outside school thereafter, will have less intellectual potential at any stage of their school career. Children who have fewer books and toys, have rarely been taken to museums or shows, who do not dance or play sport or a musical instrument will bring fewer material resources to learning, in the classroom and outside. Even the broadcast media may reduce potential if there is a 'preponderance of non-educational, entertainment viewing', which has been found to produce 'negative effects' (NRC, 2000, p151).

Children who are socialised into the variety of cultures in the UK may have the opportunity to experience a huge richness of music, dance, language, literature and art. They will have access to material resources which they can continue to bring to learning challenges in all contexts as they progress. They will already be involved in cycles of learning and will have started to learn socially by the time they start school. The question for their schools is whether the resources acquired by the children can be drawn on so as to reinforce rather than hinder their learning in the classroom. This is the issue of learning transfer, discussed later in the chapter.

If the children have not accumulated positive cultural resources from family and community which give them an expectation of success and an understanding of how to behave in the social context of school, they will not make as good progress there as their peers from middle class families. They will be unable to take full advantage of what school offers. And if home and community continue not to equip them with the cultural resources to do so, or support positively the culture and expectations of school, the gap for these children will yawn ever wider as they get older.

This is poignantly illustrated in the different lives of the two year 6 boys described in chapter 1. The son of university-educated parents clearly has the assumptions and expectations of success as part of the cultural resources he has acquired at home. But his counterpart in the special school who has spent his weekend on the floor joist is unlikely to be so equipped, although this could ultimately change if his school experiences and general circumstances are positive.

The children's linguistic resources will also vary. Understanding English is important, but so are the patterns and forms of language used between adults and children, as considered in the last chapter. The potential perplexity of children in response to conversational patterns beyond their acquaintance will disadvantage them educationally unless the classroom language forms change. The 'no language' perception (Brooker, 2002) affects children from a variety of backgrounds. Unless the linguistic resources and accomplishments of emergent bilinguals are recognised and built on in the classroom, they too will be disadvantaged.

As children get older and the influence of their peers becomes more important, they will probably also access cultural and linguistic resources from their peer culture, through stories, self-affirming narratives, music or language patterns. The role of peer culture in relation to school learning will depend upon how antithetical or supportive it is to the expectations and culture of the school.

Gender may also affect self-confidence and motivation (Arnot *et al*, 1998). The strategies employed by girls in classrooms seem to vary from those of boys, although the connection with performance is not clear. However, Arnot *et al* conclude that in general, gender identities may result from previous classroom experience – the informal outcomes of learning – and the assumptions made by teachers in structuring them (bottom box of Figure 1), rather than being culturally inherent in the gender role, separate from class or ethnic origin. In certain circumstances the articulation of masculinity has been shown to be antithetical to learning (Mac an Ghaill, 1988; Sewell, 1997; Arnot *et al*, *ibid*).

Figure 1 illustrates how children's backgrounds give them a variety of starting points for learning in school that affect their *motivation* and *self-confidence*, the likelihood of their trying more challenging learning tasks and the *strategies* they have with which to tackle them. All this has implications for their classroom success and their relative *learning disadvantage*. The challenge for schools is how to ensure that the learning accumulating outside the classroom complements and reinforces learning in school. The relationship between the two is vital.

The agenda for urban learning

Schools in many communities teach children who suffer some form of learning disadvantage, but it is only in cities that social and economic processes and the increased stratification of the school system since the 1970s have brought about concentrations of learning disadvantage in so many schools. In bottom strata schools, countering learning disadvantage is now the major educational task.

The curriculum and pedagogy appropriate in these circumstances – the agenda for urban learning – are considered in the next chapter. But first further consideration must be given to other aspects of the nature of learning and the approaches and skills required by effective learners. These should form part of the learning *resources* (see right hand box of Figure 1, p63) and ideally should be reflected in the intended formal outcomes for children from their classroom learning (see left hand box).

The nature of learning and effective learners

Learning is a diverse activity; it goes on constantly and in many contexts, in school, in the family and in the community. It takes the form of absorption of information; acquisition of knowledge; development of know-how (such as riding a bike); refinement of a skill (such as playing a musical instrument); development of understanding, alone or in combination. It may be quick or painfully slow, conscious or unconscious, even unnoticed. Learning has a variety of modes, not all of which are encountered in school settings.

At a time when much knowledge content will change beyond recognition, young people need to leave school having mastered not only the what of knowledge but also the how of acquiring it – the attributes of effective learning. Claxton (1999) describes these attributes as *resilience*, being able to bounce back from setbacks and live with the uncertainty that often accompanies learning; *resource-*

fulness, being able to choose and use a number of *strategies* for learning; and *reflectiveness*, being able to understand the processes of learning and employ alternative strategies when necessary.

Young people need to be able to engage effectively with learning and accommodate the feelings that go with it. They may experience interest or excitement, particularly after early success or encouragement from home. Or they may be discouraged by the fear of not succeeding, which could render them antagonistic to the presentation of the learning challenge itself. They may be frustrated and their previous unsuccessful learning or their learning disadvantage might undermine self-confidence and motivation. Or the subject matter may appear so arcane and so removed from their experience as to be not worth the effort.

Negative feelings of this kind are a natural accompaniment to learning and learners need to be aware of them. Learning how to allow for them is important for increasing self-efficacy and building learning strategies. The more young people can manage their feelings, the more self-confident they will be and the more motivated to engage in and take control of their learning in and after school. If they become more resilient through overcoming setbacks, their learning cycles will be positively reinforced.

Children also need the right frame of mind (Claxton, 1999): to be relaxed, even playful, so as to bring together in their minds the substance of the learning experience and what they already know. New understandings are then accommodated and new insights – or connections between different bits of knowledge or skill – are fired in the neural patternings of the brain. This process can in turn generate positive feelings which reinforce the learning. In the most developed form of this state of mind, where the conscious mind is 'quieted', imagination is more vivid, memories clearer and solutions to problems more readily apparent. They 'come to mind' more readily. This is the basis for the most creative thinking.

Achieving this is more difficult for children in bottom strata schools, who experience a greater social divide between family, community and school (Dyson and Robson, 1999). Circumstances and experiences at home may make it difficult to attend to the emotions around learning and the appropriate states of mind, particularly if children are agitated or their homes chaotic. The boy at the Bristol special school was unable to slip easily into the right frame of mind for learning on that Monday morning, and would have found it difficult to access positive feelings about his learning.

The basic processes of learning

Before learning became abstracted, as it is in schools or in literature, imitation was the way to learn a particular skill. In the modern world, it has been the basis for the traditional craft apprenticeship. Watching and trying were the key ways to learn; time at college provided more general understanding as a backdrop to the execution of practical tasks and accumulating experience. We learn many skills by being immersed in the activities which require them, for example, riding a bike or playing a musical instrument, aided by instruction from time to time.

Neither watching nor imitation are common in the school's instrumental order, but immersion is central to expressive learning. Children often learn how to behave appropriately as pupils in the classroom and as members of school communities by being immersed and corrected or coached from time to time.

The significance of these basic learning processes is that children will continue to use them in the community, particularly if craft and manual activities are prominent and they remain essential parts of children's overall repertoire as effective learners. They provide important strategies for learning which many children possess and which need to be thought about and built on by schools.

Learning to learn and Metacognition

As well as imitation or immersion, children need to be able to consciously use more complex mental processes to learn effectively in all contexts. These 'thinking skills', which make the learner more resourceful, are included in the UK national curriculum guidance (DfEE and QCA, 1999). They are specified as information-processing, reasoning, enquiry, creative thinking and evaluation, and their purpose is to ensure that 'pupils can focus on 'knowing how' as well as 'knowing what' – learning to learn' (p21 in the primary document and p23 in the secondary).

It is essential for children to master these tools for learning. They need to learn the study skill and note-taking techniques which will enable them to record, absorb and recall information, as part of information-processing and generally using their minds more effectively. They should be able to use to spider diagrams (Claxton, 1999), mind maps (Buzan, 1993) and chunking (NRC, 2000) to organise information around key concepts, and to use memory training techniques.

Learning syllogistic, inductive and other logical structures and strategies such as problem mapping will help children develop reasoning. Children should be able to 'narrow their cone of attention' consciously (Claxton, 1999, p75) to focus appropriately on the task in hand and on what is important. They need to learn whether or not they have findings which are potentially significant to their investigations. Ideally, this understanding can be extended, enabling them to distinguish what is and is not important in their lives, and learn to evaluate the consequences of what they decide or do.

To be creative, children need to learn the receptive state of mind, to quiet their conscious thinking occasionally and acquire techniques to work with others, such as brain storming, problem mapping and suspending judgement.

In addition, they need the skill of *metacognition,* proved to be key to effective learning (Bruner, 1996; Claxton, 1999; NRC, 2000). This entails being aware of one's own learning experiences and strategies; monitoring how well they have worked; deciding what approach to take to new learning challenges; explaining to oneself what has happened or has been learned; making sense of and finding meaning in learning; and setting learning goals for oneself, particularly when one has decided that one's understanding in an area is not yet adequate. As well as knowing the skills and techniques of learning, therefore, the child knows which one to apply in a given situation and when to substitute another. These processes generally work through the operation of an 'inner voice' or an 'inner conversation' (NRC, 2000, p18; Claxton, 1999).

Soft thinking skills

Children need to add soft thinking skills and techniques to their resources for learning, along with the hard thinking skills or actions of conscious thought that are so much part of the Western critical tradition. Soft forms of thinking are useful for effective learning and require a relaxed frame of mind. Children need to learn when to use their intuition when dealing with a problem or puzzle, and where it is useful to mull things over or sleep on them. Many complex problems are not susceptible to linear conscious thought whereas solutions can be generated by the 'undermind' or 'tortoise mind' (Claxton, 1997). To be fully effective learners in all domains, children need to learn how and when to quiet their minds. They need to value – and make use of – their own creativity.

A valuable soft thinking skill is *empathy*, putting oneself in the shoes of other people: peers, adults and even those long dead or fictional. Empathy can develop alongside identity, as it is constructed from the interaction between the various narratives held about oneself and the interpreted feedback received from others (Bruner, 1996). However, although some people may be naturally empathetic, the skill of putting oneself into the shoes of another can be learned and is important for behaving as an effective citizen, being a member of artificial communities like schools, and exploring history. Empathy makes it easier to learn with or from other people and be creative together. Consequently it is an important strategy for effective learning.

Learning subject knowledge

Hard and soft thinking skills will help in acquiring subject knowledge, an extremely important purpose of schooling. It is a component of the knowledge outcomes in the left hand box of Figure 1 (p63). The nature of some school subjects may be contested, but whatever the views about in whose interests they are constructed, they are vital parts of collective meaning-making in any society. Even when subject name and content change, the new information will only be understood in the light of what went before.

To master a body of knowledge means learning its conceptual structure, guiding principles, constructs and laws. Otherwise, all one sees is numerous unrelated pieces of content knowledge, to be recalled for examinations and which become redundant after leaving formal education (NRC, 2000). To begin to understand the conceptual structure of a subject, children need to be able to tackle some of it in depth, develop their own concepts and evolve a mental framework for accommodating new concepts within the discipline. A framework of this kind becomes another key resource for further learning in the subject.

Developing such a mental framework takes time and cannot be hurried. But it is more effective than covering a subject broadly but shallowly (NRC, 2000), even though this might be encouraged by detailed statutory curriculum requirements. For effective learning, depth is better than breadth.

As children develop their conceptual grasp, it is vital that their understanding is monitored through formative feedback (Black and Wiliam, 1998; NRC, 2000), to ensure that they do indeed understand and appreciate the structure of the knowledge concerned. Otherwise they may go up blind alleys and acquire misconceptions which can be difficult to shake, thus impeding further understanding (NRC, 2001). In Vygotskian terms (1986), it is important that children are effectively and skilfully supported across each step of their potential learning, or across their *zone of proximal development* (Figure 1) – what the children could learn with assistance that other people know now. This requires *scaffolding*, a key *assistance to learning*, discussed in the next chapter.

Transferring and applying learning

It is also important that young people learn the transferability of their knowledge as they acquire it. Learning is bound up with the context in which it takes place – its location, time of day, physical conditions and the feelings or states of mind of the learner at the time (Claxton, 1999; NRC, 2000). To be useful, however, it needs to be capable of being used in other contexts and situations, and the good learner needs to be able to recognise its relevance and apply it. The highly artificial, ritualised context of the school may sometimes be a hindrance to effective transfer of this sort. It is no accident that many people find it difficult to remember many of the things they were taught at school, especially when they were crammed or drilled for examination purposes, or the knowledge was remote from their everyday lives.

This has implications for young people's learning. Hard and soft thinking skills are best developed within the context of other learning, for example subject knowledge or the development of practical skills. If thinking skills are learned merely in the abstract, they will remain wrapped in their abstract trappings and the learner will not see the relevance of their application elsewhere – the brain will not fire in the appropriate way. These thinking skills are best learned within the context of more than one school subject or knowledge structure, to aid their cross-application or transfer. Inquiry, for example, is an identified and knowable skill in both science and history which could be specifically taught in both. Seeing connections, often intuitively, and applying learning in this way is essential for acquiring knowledge.

As children learn new concepts in a body of subject knowledge, they need to discuss how these will be recalled and used. There are techniques to aid this process, such as reciprocal teaching whereby young people explain ideas or facts to their peers or engage in 'what-if' thinking to sharpen their mental processes (NRC, 2000).

Some of the contextual situations in which acquired knowledge needs to be applied might need to be practised or created artificially, particularly when they are beyond the experience or understanding of the children, or remote from school life. For example, schools place much emphasis on individual abstract reasoning, whereas the world outside generally deals in contextual reasoning, such as how to get shopping home from the supermarket when you do not live on a bus route. Similarly, the exercise of group intelligence (Claxton, 1997) is essential in some occupational settings such as a warship, research laboratory or restaurant kitchen, but unusual in others. So learning should be practised in different groupings – pairs, groups, whole classes, year groups, whole schools, and communities. Learning thinking techniques to support work in these groupings, such as De Bono's six hats (1986), brainstorming, or force field analysis also aids transfer.

Tools to aid and support learning

Tools are important. They are used to 'off-load mental effort', as Claxton puts it (1999, p214) and their purpose is to enable learning or thinking to reach a conclusion faster or more effectively. Some of them, the so-called 'internal tools' (*ibid*) are the thinking skills, or knowing how to learn, already analysed.

There are also the familiar external tools for learning – abacus, calculator, drawing board, tape recorder and so on. The most significant and potentially powerful are available through information and communications technology. Computers, with their huge processing capacity, provide a variety of problem-solving tools, produce projections, analyse complex problems or data, provide access to masses of information very quickly and enable feedback on the execution of certain tasks. They are a superb support for self-directed and self-efficacious learning, therefore, and for metacognition. Effective learners need to have access to computers and be shown how to use them. Access to a computer outside school is a huge advantage and increases the effectiveness of transfer. This is less likely in the homes of the children attending bottom strata schools, though this may be changing.

Other barriers to children's learning in bottom strata schools

Chapter 4 discussed the sorts of barrier to learning and teaching which could arise from the context of bottom strata schools and this chapter has looked at cumulative learning disadvantage, drawing on a social model of learning (Figure 1). Before considering how schools should respond to their context and the curriculum and pedagogy which are appropriate in bottom strata schools, we need to note certain additional barriers to children's achievement which are endemic within the education profession and its conceptions of children, and the nature of teaching.

Notions of fixed ability

Categorising children, sometimes on the basis of misconceptions of their level of functioning, creates a barrier to their learning. Such categorisation has a long and persistent history in the UK – Jackson (1964) describes it as it operated in 1960s. The system of secondary schools set up after the Second World War depended on it. The tests used to allocate places rested on the widely held assumption that all children could be accurately categorised by the age of eleven. The notion that intelligence was measurable, irrespective of background, 'dominated a generation of educational thinking' (Crook *et al,* 1999, p10/11).

The notion of 'ability' as somehow fixed for life has persisted long after the end of formal selection for secondary school, especially in the UK. In comparing English and French primary schools, for example, the *Quest* project (Broadfoot *et al,* 2000) found that while English teachers and children considered that success came from ability as fixed in the child, in France effort was considered more important. French teachers made the assumption that children would and could achieve certain minimum standards if they worked hard enough.

Gillborn and Youdell (2000) found that teachers in the English schools they studied held to a notion of fixed ability, which they felt was indicated by children's measured attainment. In the context of a working class school, it was considered natural that the children would attain less because of their social background. This was a clear case of lowered expectations or, as Thomson (2002) describes it in the Australian context, of taking the limiting 'This school ... These kids... This community' view – what can one expect?'

The process of ascribing fixed ability and then having fixed expectations as a consequence, is described by Claxton (1999):

> .... the word 'ability' is used as a synonym for 'intelligence', and is taken to refer to some inner resource which accounts for actual performance ... Phrases such as 'ability level', 'high ability', 'less able' and so on are used to denote a real, personal characteristic which is generally fixed, limiting, pervasive, predictive, monolithic, measurable and valuable. (p28/9)

This view of fixed ability and the notion of intelligence as an innate measurable quantity have been discredited for some time. Claxton (1999) quotes Michael Howe:

> .....there are no strong grounds for believing that identification of someone's measured intelligence justifies any meaningful statement about that individual's qualities, achievements or attributes. (p32)

The notion of intellectual and physical potential being a constituent of identity, as in Figure 1, is a more dynamic concept. It recognises the role and importance of previous learning and personal history. Allied to the notion of future potential contained in the zone of proximal development (Vygotsky, 1986), it is the basis for a positive approach to further learning and development, instead of making assumptions about how far children can go. Children's achievement is not predetermined, as Hallam (2002) makes clear:

> Researchers now acknowledge that learning outcomes and performance depend on the complex interactions of many factors, including the characteristics of the learning situation, motivation, effort, belief in the possibility of success, opportunity, knowledge of learning strategies, self-awareness and prior knowledge, in addition to ability. (p4)

In addition to the disadvantages children in bottom strata schools may bring to learning, the notions held about them can further limit their achievement, as Gillborn and Youdell (2000) demonstrate.

The notion of a fixed quantum of ability will be equally harmful if held by the children themselves, as they will believe that their competence cannot be increased. If they believe their innate ability is high, they become merely interested in giving a good account of themselves and receiving positive feedback, but are unlikely to stretch themselves, as they think they cannot improve their capacity to learn (NRC, 2000, p102). And children who believe their innate ability is low become resigned to not doing well and develop strategies to minimise the importance of their self-perceived incompetence. This is a significant problem in bottom strata schools, particularly after cyclically repeated unsuccessful learning. The 'locus of control' (NRC, 2000, p294) has in both cases been passed to someone else.

Children who believe that their competence can be increased (NRC, 2000) can take responsibility for their own learning, select more challenging tasks and develop their self-efficacy. They are less inclined to be worried about making mistakes, so are more resilient learners. Interestingly, Broadfoot *et al* (2000) found that French teachers were much more severe about school work than English teachers were, but because French children did not see this as personal criticism of something they could not alter, they took it as a matter of course. They could stop their teachers' criticism by working harder.

The possible limitations of alternative conceptions of intelligence
Since the view of intelligence as something innate and measurable has become discredited, alternative conceptualisations have emerged, but these too may be limiting for children in bottom strata schools.

Howard Gardner's (1985) concept of multiple intelligences has been highly influential. The notion that children can be good at more than one thing while not being good at others has had a great symbolic power for many teachers, replacing the notion of the 'unchangeable intellect' as Gardner describes it. The National Research Council describes the application of multiple intelligences to classrooms as a 'grass roots movement ... only just beginning' (NRC, 2000, p101).

There is immense interest in Gardner's eight intelligences – linguistic, mathematical/logical, spatial, musical, bodily kinaesthetic, inter-personal, intra-personal and naturalist. They are explained and enthused on by publications popularising developments in our understanding of the brain and their implications for learning, such as Dryden and Vos (1994), Jensen (1995), Smith (1996) and Rose and Nicholl (1997).

The use of multiple intelligences is often related to an individual's preferred ways of learning, based on their own particular intelligence profiles. On the website of the University of the First Age, for example, a popular national organisation in the UK devoted to spreading good learning practice based on research, the explanation of multiple intelligences is framed completely in these terms. The notion of preferred ways of learning – or learning styles — has become popular. These styles can be described as visual, auditory or kinaesthetic (Smith, 1996) and an individual's learning is likely to be most effective in one of them. Jensen (1995) details four other models for describing learning styles.

This is not the place to undertake a detailed critique of these notions. Their strength has been that they have encouraged teachers to take a wider view of what might be happening in their classrooms and what their pupils might be able to do with the right stimulus. But in a curious way, individual learners are absent from many of these accounts of learning, except as various congeries of preferences or styles, or as recipients (*tabula rasa?*) of brain-based (but context-free) techniques, which may be sound enough in themselves. What makes individuals unique – their potential to learn from past experience; the material, cultural and linguistic resources they have accumulated; and their learning stance and strategies – is not taken into account. Yet it is this uniqueness that has to be the starting point for the learning experiences provided by schools if they are to be designed appropriately around the children. This is doubly so in bottom strata schools, where individuals' uniqueness may disadvantage them in learning terms and in the recognition of their true potential.

There is a real danger that detailed profiles of learning styles compiled for individuals on the basis of questionnaires or exercises become as fixed a basis for deciding what will engage and excite them as notions of fixed intelligence or ability. If children are identified as having strengths in the bodily-kinaesthetic intelligence, or as kinaesthetic learners, then the danger is that this is how they will be provided for, instead of being given sufficient opportunity to develop their capabilities and learn in other ways. They might spend a lot of their time in movement.

Children do change as a consequence of learning and their wider experiences. The real barrier to their learning is the belief that they do not.

Emotional Intelligence

Finally, there is the concept of *emotional intelligence* advocated by Goleman (1996) as an alternative to general cognitive views of ability. He has advocated learning in five domains of emotional intelligence that he defined as: knowing one's emotions; managing emotions; motivating oneself; recognising emotions in others; and handling relationships (*ibid* p43). Managing negative emotions is clearly essential in the learning context as they may prevent engagement. But emotional literacy, as it has become known, might also be important in other contexts such as managing behaviour or conflict, considerable issues in bottom strata schools.

The notion of emotional intelligence is not necessarily a fixed or limiting one, and may be a useful concept for developing an important aspect of potential. It needs to be considered for the curriculum and pedagogy of bottom strata schools.

Chapter 6

The curriculum and pedagogy of bottom strata schools

This chapter considers some of the general characteristics of teaching and then discusses curriculum and pedagogy in relation to bottom strata schools.

The unpredictability of the classroom

Classrooms are complex places. Children step into them as unique individuals, with their own physical and intellectual potential, and their own personal combinations of material, cultural and linguistic resources. They bring particular stances to learning, which may be affected either way by events in or out of school on a particular day. And they bring their own strategies for learning, as we have seen, but they find them difficult to use in certain lessons because they were learned in a different context.

Teachers, as Fullan (2001a) says, 'experience students as individuals in specific circumstances who are being influenced by multiple and differing forces for which generalisations are not possible' (p32/3). No matter what the format, approach or intention of a lesson, its processes will engage uniquely with the individual starting point of each child present. There will be as many versions of the lesson going on as there are children, even when they are expected to be working on the same thing. Or as Ayers (2001) says, in the tenth of his twelve myths of teaching:

> Teachers sometimes assume that there is only one true story of classroom life ... In reality, teachers know one story of what's going on, but not

> the only story nor even the 'true story.' True stories are multitudinous be-
> cause there are thirty-some true stories. Kids are active interpreters of
> classroom reality and their interpretations are only sometimes synony-
> mous with their teacher's interpretations. (p15/16)

From the teacher's point of view, whatever the similarities between
groups of children, lessons take their own paths, with their own
unique moments, many unpredictable, reflecting the particular combination of young minds in the room at the time. Teachers get to
know these combinations as school years progress:

> ... teachers refer often to the personality or character of a class, insisting
> that cohorts along with their parents are often different from one year to
> the next and respond to different treatments. (Huberman, 1983, p486)

This means that what has worked perfectly well with one group of
children may not always work quite as well – or at all – with another,
and the reason may not be clear:

> Teachers can never be sure of the reasons why a curriculum component
> works or 'bombs out', or why one timid child becomes more expressive
> as the year goes on and an apparently similar case the following year is
> unresponsive to the same techniques. (*ibid*, p486)

Teaching therefore, has unpredictable and uncertain aspects, and
even when being driven by national expectations and varying
degrees of prescription, it has to be deeply rooted in a day to day
practicality.

What is required from teachers in the face of this variability and
occasional uncertainty is that they run their classrooms flexibly,
keep an open mind about what is happening in front of them as they
teach and, most of all, be prepared to learn from their experiences
and those of their colleagues. Teachers as well as pupils need to be
skilled learners.

Teachers as learners

Teachers learn in many different ways about the development and
improvement of their classroom practice and everything associated
with it. After initial training, they continue to learn from their everyday experience of teaching children, a process of informal learning
by which they absorb and accumulate what often becomes tacit
knowledge, usually drawn on and added to intuitively.

Teachers also participate in more formal learning through the availability of school closure days, training associated with national initiatives, training in their developing responsibilities, or accredited higher degree programmes in universities. They may also participate in research projects. If this more formal, often de-contextualised, learning is to be incorporated into the specific circumstances of their classrooms, however, some process of reflection is required. Teachers also reflect on their informal learning, but less systematically and often as part of their metacognitive processes.

The processes of informal learning

Newly qualified teachers begin work without much informal learning, other than that accumulated during supervised practice periods in schools as part of their initial training. Beside the formal knowledge content of their training, they will also have learned some basic routines of preparing classrooms for children and thinking about and preparing particular lessons. As they teach, their experience begins to accumulate. They learn how children react to being spoken to in certain ways, how to call for attention effectively, and how to handle some of the detailed issues of classroom and lesson organisation which can only come from experience. They begin to learn how long what they have prepared for children will actually take to complete, and they will find themselves with too much or too little prepared. They begin to see the results of their teaching in the work children produce for them, and they learn the 'character' or 'personality' of their classes or groups of children, as Huberman observed (1983).

They will absorb some of these experiences without reflection. They learn how to carry themselves, the appropriate body language and the tones of voice to use without having to think. These enable their classrooms to remain calm and the children to be confident. They begin to develop a sense of what is happening in the class as a whole, even when they are engaged in working with a group of children. They can assess a class as soon as they walk into a room – they know whether something is awry or not. Headteachers, especially primary heads, learn to sense their schools like this as they walk round the buildings.

When incidents or unanticipated interruptions occur, therefore, the experienced teacher knows intuitively what to do. They take a 'reading' of the situation, as Atkinson and Claxton (2000) call it. They recognise a pattern and respond to it, as there is usually no time for cool reflection. These patterns – in the behaviour and sounds coming from groups of children – are complex and can only be fully absorbed subconsciously, just like the complex problems to which Claxton referred (1999).

Even as the secondary school deputy head approaches a large group of 16 year old boys at the back of the school sports hall at lunch time, she is absorbing signs and signals in the seconds she has to prepare herself for intervention, without thinking consciously about how she knows. Where in the group is the incident, she is thinking, how many boys are directly involved, how many are spectators and how many can I ask to leave, and so on. As a deputy head and a repository of the authority of the school, she cannot afford to get it wrong; the boys' previous experience of her interventions may begin to do her job for her anyway – they may disperse as she approaches. Mission accomplished.

This sense of what is happening in classrooms – or corridors or playgrounds – is often described as *withitness* (Kounin, 1970) or, as the children themselves might say, having eyes in the back of the head. Experienced and skilled teachers just know – they do not have to analyse.

In a 1999 study in Bristol schools, withitness was identified as an important quality for the management of behaviour in the urban classroom, where unpredictable events often occur. The study was undertaken by trainee educational psychologists who wished to identify the common characteristics of successful urban teachers in bottom strata schools. Their study (Major *et al*, 1999) used a schedule to examine the teaching of thirteen 'outstanding teachers' identified for them by the local education authority advisory service.

Reflective learning

Much formal training for teachers also becomes absorbed as tacit knowledge, subsequently to be drawn on intuitively as the basis for further learning. Experienced primary teachers, for example, once they had grasped the mechanics of the literacy hour required by the UK national literacy strategy, were able to access their understanding on a daily basis and begin to concentrate on what was or was not working with their own children.

Any change in classrooms involves some process of trialling and reflection because of the unique connections with the 'thirty-some' children in each class (Ayers, 2001). This is true whether the need to try something different or differently has been identified by the individual teacher, the department or school, or by national government. There have been many representations of the processes involved. The attraction of the particular model illustrated on page 87 (Figure 2), from the *Fifth Discipline Fieldbook* for schools (Senge *et al*, 2000), is that it shows change more realistically as a spiral process, rather than as incessantly going round the same circle. Nothing works completely as intended the first time, of course; improvements need to be worked on; with an open mind and a disposition to get better each time, every turn of the cycle adds cumulatively to knowledge, improving quality. Classroom improvement and teacher learning about it are closely related.

Learning cycles vary, but those that are going to be effective will have the sorts of features shown in the model, even if not explicitly. A cycle must begin with a *revisit/clarify goals and purposes* stage, whereby the need for something different is thought about, even if identified from outside the school. Then comes the *plan* stage to ensure that a change can be put into place in a classroom in the *take action/experiment* stage. As the change is being implemented, it is necessary to *assess/gather evidence* about it, even if only intuitively, so that it is possible to *study/reflect/evaluate* (on) it. This makes it possible to *modify actions* for next time the particular change is to be used, and this will be preceded by a *revisit/clarify* goals stage to ensure the next *plan* is adequate.

Like all learning, such reflective cycles or turns of the spiral can be quick or slow. They can cover an individual lesson, for example, or a week of a scheme of work. A turn of the spiral can start at any place. The identification of behavioural or other issues could start in the *assess/gather evidence* stage, if a lesson is being observed as the basis for future coaching. A need for something different could be identified at the *take action/experiment* stage, if informal intuitive appreciation of classroom events suggests it. Or the process could start at the *study/reflect/evaluate* stage, perhaps in response to training or an external input.

Fostering reflective teacher learning

As reflection is a process of learning, it can be helped and stimulated in certain ways.

Because learning is an interactive process between the learner and the environment, as we saw in the last chapter, it is best for the learner to have some control of the learning processes, even if the need for learning is decided elsewhere. Taking control of learning is as important for adults as it is for children. Learning needs to be at an appropriate pace; the learner needs to be able to draw the right lessons from practice and to accommodate the learning into what they already know. The danger with innovations developed outside the classroom that are not accompanied by this reflective process is that they become absorbed as drills, limiting the possibilities for further development, adaptation or improvement.

It is helpful to work with colleagues rather than in the isolation of the teacher's own room, although classroom doors do tend to be open more these days. Teaching needs to change in response to changes in the children and the learning context. Sometimes classroom practice can become *routinised* as the result of teachers' long experience and extensive informal learning (Pollard with Filer, 1996). The pupils themselves may collude with the teacher to reduce the intensity of their learning challenge (*ibid*). In all such circumstances, colleagues can be helpful. Observation or discussion, perhaps arising from the monitoring of teaching by senior staff, can draw attention to things that are not obvious to the teachers themselves. However, where observation is being used as part of a reflective cycle to help bring about improvement, this must be kept distinct from monitoring for accountability. Monitoring by itself brings about no improvement.

Beyond learning from their immediate colleagues, teachers need access to knowledge and good practice from other schools, to avoid the school as a whole becoming routinised or isolated. If schools are

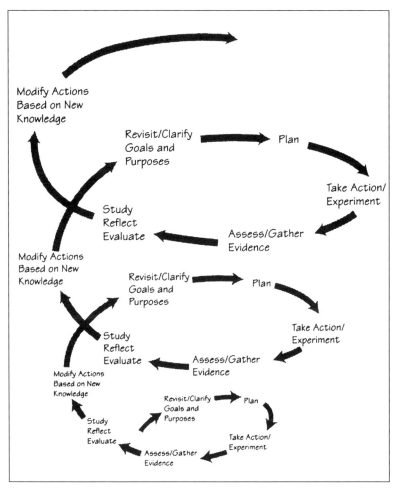

Figure 2: Reflective learning and improvement as a spiral process. From Senge et al (2000) p190

going to be able to collaborate with each other to enable such an exchange of knowledge, they have to develop some degree of mutuality. This may be facilitated by a university or a local education authority who can point to where teachers and schools may learn.

Reflective learning is itself a skilled process for both teacher and observer. Teachers need time to develop and practise their skills and develop their metacognition, or 'meta-learning', as Stoll *et al* (2003) call it. This makes both learning and the improvement of classrooms a conscious and deliberate process, which is what a learning school requires.

Although reflective learning should certainly be part of the natural activity of teaching this does place extra demands on teachers at a time when workload is a problematic issue and the main cause of teachers leaving the profession (Smithers and Robinson, 2001). Nonetheless, there must be a positive professional expectation in schools that teachers do reflect on their practice even if this is seen as 'pressure'. Fullan (2001a) is clear about the need for pressure to complement support for teachers and schools if improvement is to take place, but this does not mean it has to be punitive.

Wider reflective cycles and professional learning communities
Reflective cycles can cover periods longer than the individual lesson and involve far more staff than the individual teacher. So if schools are encouraging reflective practice, it makes sense for teachers across year groups or faculties or even whole schools to share their work and help each other improve. The *revisit/clarify goals and purposes* stage of the cycle could be run collegially; the *assess/gather* evidence stage could take place across a number of classroom settings for various age groups and subjects. There could be joint *planning* to enable teachers to access information about good practice from colleagues, including teachers from other schools. Sharing the burden can reduce the pressure.

When this happens across a school, it becomes the *professional learning community* essential for improvement (Fullan, 2001a). The research, as he says, shows that 'collegiality, as measured by the frequency of communication, mutual support (and) help' (p124) is a strong indicator of the successful implementation of change. Just as teachers must have their own reflective cycles, they must also find their own meaning in any change. There is no substitute for the 'primacy of personal contact'. This enables reflection and subsequent improvement.

Whether the objective is small scale change or the initiation of longer term classroom-based research, teachers need to be learners and they will find this easiest in professional learning communities or learning schools.

Teaching for Learning

Learning schools are always engaged in the consideration and exploration of learning and its implications for classrooms and children, from first thing in the morning until they close. All their processes need to be considered from this standpoint and focused to maximise the potential and the resources gained by the pupils.

Effective engagement with learning – beginning with the environment

Children's preparation for learning needs to begin when they enter the building. Schools need to evoke the positive feelings and states of mind which accompany effective learning. The environment must be welcoming. It should calm and relax children, perhaps by sensitive colour schemes and background noise or music. It needs to enable children to make immediate connections between what is important to them – their own interests, the dominant imagery and symbols of their families and communities – and life inside school. They need to see and hear these connections (NRC, 1999) as soon as they walk into school, otherwise they will find some of the notions with which they are presented in the classroom difficult to accept (*ibid*), and certainly to transfer (NRC, 2000; Claxton, 1999). At the same time, the building should advertise on its walls and in its displays what the business of learning involves in that school – the strategies involved – and the characteristics of effective learners.

The expressive order of the school – its dress, rituals and expectations – needs to be designed around supporting learning, not a 're-invigorated traditionalism' emphasising artificial differences between school and community, or what some adults may think appropriate for children. It must be clearly supportive, particularly at secondary school, of young people negotiating their way round a complex social structure unlike anything they have experienced before. Relations between staff and pupils, and between younger and older pupils, need to be modelled in relation to learning and not context-free views of authority.

Even with the complex logistics of moving large numbers around the site several times a day, there are ways of softening the impact and helping pupils orientate themselves for learning. Longer learning times with allowance for breaks can help, together with flexibility at the end of sessions instead of the regimentation of bells. Classrooms need to be fit for purpose. Besides the appropriate equipment, thought needs to be given to colour schemes and background music there too. Where possible, appropriate furniture, size of room and environment should cater for the variety of learning groups and potential types of learning.

Making connections in the classroom

In the classroom, the teachers need to understand the implications of the children's potential, resources, learning stance and strategies for their starting points for learning. They need to create and use language patterns and behaviour norms in the classroom the children find comfortable and conducive to learning. Although discomfort may not be obvious, it may significantly reduce learning and thus lower expectations.

Learning to learn: practising hard and soft thinking strategies

General learning strategies, or thinking skills, are already included in National Curriculum documentation (DfEE and QCA, 1999). The intended formal outcomes for classroom learning in the school need to reflect these general learning strategies and the school must be clear how they will be covered across the curriculum and where. Pupils need to understand this too. Some skills and strategies will be covered in many areas; some may require specific teaching and then be practised in a variety of contexts. For example, in learning about a new topic in any subject, children should be encouraged to try some of the information-processing techniques discussed in the last chapter and evaluate their usefulness at the end of the lesson, alongside their developing subject knowledge. These techniques thus become resources for learning.

Young people should be encouraged to be reflective learners and to develop their metacognition *en route* to taking control of their learning. Specific attention could also be given to developing metacognitive skills out of context, then using them in subject-related learning. Teachers, as learners, should make it clear to their pupils what strategies they themselves use as part of this process and encourage some of the characteristics of effective learners by modelling them. The strategies should be referred to by name and in displays. Children should learn that it is acceptable to make mistakes and be resilient about it.

Opportunities to practise soft thinking skills should be explored. There are many areas where the development of empathy can be considered, encouraging the relaxed state of mind in which intuition can be listened to and hunches examined. The importance of taking pressure off children at least some of the time needs to be considered and discussed with pupils.

The shape of lessons needs to be varied over a year – and at secondary level this might require coming off timetable. Pupils need to be able to work for long periods on particular learning tasks, if appropriate, instead of the usual stop-start-go, and they need to be able to learn in groups of different sizes, to enable collective cognition. Again, the reasoning for all this needs to be made clear to the pupils.

Formal teaching in subjects

Subject teachers in both sectors should include the key learning strategies or skills in the formal outcomes for their lessons, alongside the subject requirements of the national curriculum or literacy and numeracy strategies. For subject knowledge, children also need help in developing the mental models described in the last chapter, the conceptual frameworks they need to improve their understanding. The key concepts and a map of them need to be advertised and displayed and the children reminded of them to help them navigate their way round the subject.

Teachers also need to ensure they probe and are clear about the current stages of children's understanding, seeking feedback from them frequently in a variety of ways (NRC, 2000). They can 'scaffold' children's learning – that is, provide assistance in bridging their zone of proximal development (Vygotsky, 1986), to the next stage of what they could learn – by making tasks interesting, keeping a focus on the advertised goal of learning, making the steps simpler by breaking tasks down, enabling pupils to control feelings about the learning and choose relevant learning strategies or thinking skills, and ensuring the children understand what the goal, on the other side of the zone, looks like (NRC, 2000).

Teaching for transfer and applicability

The process of formal teaching includes time spent on enabling pupils to apply their learning in other contexts. If teaching emphasises 'memorisation as an end in itself' or students 'learn(ing) to solve problems by following formulas' (NRC, 1999, p26) then the knowledge gained will seldom be applied.

Children need the time to practise where their new knowledge may be applied. This means thinking about the transfer of learning in the context of their community and other experiences, not just the subject structures. If the subject remains arcane or divorced from the everyday reality of peer group, family and community, success is unlikely. Relevance or applicability need to be planned for. The subject needs to be explained in terms to which the pupils can relate.

Overcoming barriers

Finally, learning schools which teach for learning need to be open-minded about what their pupils can and might achieve. Although the reality of expectations driven by performance targets cannot be ignored, nor the priority of working with children currently at risk of not making benchmark scores, the pursuit of an agenda for learning such as suggested here is much wider than the current agenda.

Teaching for urban learning

Everything in this chapter could apply to schools in any context. All schools and classrooms could improve; all children need to acquire the appropriate strategies to bring to their learning, inside school and out. All teachers need to be learners and all schools learning organisations. All classrooms are complex places, although those in bottom strata schools are likely to be more so. And the extent of the learning disadvantage found there makes overcoming it urgent, to prevent disadvantage continuing throughout school careers and into adult life.

If learning disadvantage is to be addressed, all the factors which give rise to it – at each stage of the learning cycle – must receive attention and their implications for teaching considered. If children start from behind, they must have a real opportunity and time to catch up. The curriculum and pedagogy of bottom strata schools thus need to have a distinctive character, although schools by themselves cannot make all the difference and the curriculum needs to extend far beyond classrooms into the wider community. Mutual transfer between school and community is vitally important, as is the learning itself with which the children need to be equipped.

The curriculum and pedagogy of bottom strata schools

Connecting with the children

Making effective connections, so that learning may commence and be effective, is a major challenge for bottom strata schools and must begin long before the probing of pupils' understanding and the attractive display of learning strategies. It is especially important that the classroom and school context are designed to enable the pupils to feel comfortable and prepare them adequately for learning. The signs, symbols, rituals and significant rhythms of family and community life are likely to be quite different from those automatically assumed in the context of the school. In some bottom strata schools, a great many different languages will be spoken, some of the population will be transient and significant numbers of children will be vulnerable to racism. Even if there is no ethnic or religious diversity, there will be class differences and the associated differences in expectations. The signs and symbols pupils bring will be diverse and these differences need to be carefully researched so that all children can make the mental transition from their lives outside school to learning inside.

The young people in bottom strata schools come from homes and communities with language patterns and codes which differ from those of the school and classroom, even if English is their first language, to which linguistic context they return each day. The conversational patterns between children and adults, or adolescents and adults, may take different forms from those assumed in school, reflecting differing generational roles and modes of learning. If the convention of one set of adults holding and transmitting knowledge is at odds with that of the community, children may find it difficult to accept the norms of the classroom and how learning is framed. This difficulty may increase as the pupils get older.

Moll and Greenberg (1992) contrasted the ritualised modes of learning in the classroom with the learning largely by imitation in the social context of a poor working class Hispanic community. This meant that the children's learning in the community could not be drawn on and built upon by learning in school. This was true both for the content of their learning (eg how to change the oil in a car), and the process used to acquire it (watching and imitating, a basic process of learning). Moll and Greenberg say it is important for teachers to be able to draw on the *funds of knowledge* in the community into which children have been initiated, in order to promote the most effective learning in school. These funds of knowledge exist in every community and consist of the understandings which underpin living and working, together with the communication networks from which children as well as adults draw their meaning.

Schools need to draw on community content and process contexts so that teaching is seen by pupils as relevant and immediate. They must incorporate appropriate signs and symbols into the teaching environment to enable effective transition from the patterns of language use outside school. Only thus will they draw in the children effectively and create expectations that will support pupils' learning in school.

Enrolling the community

Children will be more receptive when the real context of the community is used as a platform for school learning. It is the building block on which to base transition to more formal knowledge domains and other forms of learning. In the Moll and Greenberg research (1992), the children studied construction, which was a large employer in the community. The teachers involved parents in providing some of the input to the school work and planning how it would be done. In a separate example, a teacher concerned about a child's writing asked her to undertake a more challenging piece of work on a topic of direct interest to her. How can the equivalent be done in the UK?

The community itself and, as they get older, the children, can provide the best tutors for ensuring that the school reflects local context, and helps pupils make an effective mental transition to formal learning. Drawing the community into the activities and priorities of the school will not only help reduce the 'otherness' of the school for children, it will make clear the connecting links for them. This could be by recruiting 'teaching associates', in Barber's (1996a) words, or members of the community contributing to some programmes, such as in the Moll and Greenberg example. Teaching assistants and certainly governors need to be drawn from the community.

Enrolling parents

It is essential that parents be enrolled effectively in supporting the learning and development of their children. Research confirms common sense in showing that parents from even the most deprived backgrounds want their children to do well. The parents living in poverty researched for the ATD Fourth World study (2000), for example, were clear that education was the one way their children could avoid continuing the cycle of poverty, but most parents had not been effectively enrolled by the school and most could not support their children's learning effectively and feel they were full partners in their education. There are cultural issues here too, but this might be addressed by providing routine parent workshop-style events, perhaps jointly led by parents, significant members of the community and school staff. Regular two-way exchanges between staff and parents, perhaps with groups of parents facilitated by the governing body, might also help, but this again will depend on the context. Effective communications need to be worked on – remember the negative honeymoons experienced by new heads in some communities.

Reflecting community and parental aspirations

The community and the parents should be enrolled into the aspirations and mission of the school. This is more than consulting the community on the vision of the staff, rubber-stamped by the governors. It means reflecting the aspirations brought by the community, with the community able to see the school as contributing to their aspirations for themselves and their children. It means making attempts to reduce the 'divide' and the potential 'cultural imperialism' of the staff that parents sometimes complain about (Dyson and Robson, 1999).

Staff, particularly teachers, should be recruited where possible from ethnic minority and working class backgrounds, so that it is in balance with the pupil population and not dominated by a monocultural perspective. Schools need staff who are able to start from where the children are without making major mental adjustments. These are the teachers who will instinctively be able to tell you that they 'understand these kids' and that they 'know what they are talking about'.

Because of the potential divide between school on the one hand and community and parents on the other, there must also be mechanisms in place for more regular dialogue on more general issues than learning. A regular forum with the governors may be appropriate, but this will need to vary with the context. More than one forum may be necessary in schools serving diverse communities, with appropriate interpreters present.

Enrolling the children

It may seem to teenagers that the whole adult world is conspiring to make them accept their values and learn what they want them to know. It is! But developing distinct differences between themselves and adults is an important part of growing up and acquiring their own identities. The danger is that the identities generated from peer cultures and promoted through the media may be anti-learning.

Identity is fundamental to learning. Matters that concern young people require attention, as they may well reflect discontent in the wider community, such as institutional racism. There are several studies of successful work in schools to combat racism (Gillborn, 1995). Schools should make it clear which signs and symbols of peer group culture are acceptable in school, for example, the hairstyles discussed by Sewell (1997), and their relation to the encouragement of learning. Above all, the young people need to be asked for their views, whether by people with 'neutral' outsider roles, possibly researchers, as in the Blatchford (1996) study, but also, and regularly, by staff in the school, perhaps through the mechanisms of a school council and the governors. Then these views need to be acted on; for example, the lessons they find really boring should be changed. The students should become willing and able to contribute to the mission of the school.

There are no simple answers to counteracting the 'keener' culture. It has to be approached pragmatically and in light of the specific backgrounds of the pupils. Some schools appear to be effectively enrolling certain of the signs, symbols and trappings of young people's interests as part of their peer culture: working with mobile phone companies for instance, or giving tickets for the cinema or fast food outlets as positive rewards. Awards evenings or celebrations might be held in night clubs, with the adults disappearing when the formal proceedings are over.

Developing children as self-confident and resourceful learners

The goal of developing young people as self-confident, resourceful lifelong learners with high degrees of self-efficacy, needs to be the basis of classroom work. Only then can pupils be adequately prepared for life in the constantly changing society of the twenty-first century, or for taking control of their own learning and lives.

Even when a basis of trust has been established and children begin to make an effective mental transition into school with their parents' support, those in bottom strata schools will still be less likely to approach learning with self-confidence or motivation. They may find it difficult to sustain their engagement with the norms and expectations of school, even after the incorporation of community funds of knowledge. Many children, especially if they are experiencing social and material deprivation, will still have low levels of self-esteem and self-efficacy and find it difficult to concentrate or take learning seriously.

Learning success in the classroom is the only way to counteract learning disadvantage. Positive learning cycles need to be established early in pupils' school careers and be continually reinforced until they become self-sustaining. Especially in bottom strata schools, pupils need to be equipped with the general tools to help them engage and succeed with learning, despite all the other distractions in their lives. Teachers have to work explicitly, and appropriately according to age, on children's engagement with learning, their hard and soft thinking skills including metacognition, development of conceptual frameworks for subjects and the application and transfer of learning in the major knowledge domains.

Particularly because of where they come from, the children need the ability to navigate their way through the uncertainty and unpleasant feelings which sometimes accompany their learning. They need to challenge themselves and be more ambitious in their objectives, using the tools, skills and strategies acquired. They need to work on their increasingly self-set objectives as they take greater control. They need help with visualising and taking appropriate steps towards their objectives, choosing the skills and strategies as they go, so must receive individual feedback.

Through continuing success, children become more conscious of their own learning and what they know. They become more skilled at choosing strategies or mental tools to tackle new learning challenges and become better at reviewing or changing those which are inappropriate. They learn to articulate to themselves how they make these choices, perhaps first out loud and then silently. They thus become mindful of their inner processes and thereby skilled at metacognition. In these inner conversations with themselves, they become reflective learners.

If these goals were achieved by pupils in bottom strata schools, they could ultimately develop their capacity to combat their potential learning disadvantage themselves.

Developing self-efficacy and learning transfer into the community

The growth in self-confidence, motivation and self-belief resulting from learning success brings the possibility in the right conditions of widening self-efficacy beyond school. The processes of achieving, reviewing and re-setting objectives in the learning context could be transferred into the community, but only if these processes were learned in school with a view to such use. If hard and soft thinking skills are to become part of a community's funds of knowledge, time for what if thinking is needed to allow children to consider their effective transfer, and opportunities in the community available to practise the skills in a wider context. One way would be to take aspects of the community as the subject for study in appropriate parts of the curriculum, as in Moll and Greenberg's example, and to locate the classroom or workshop for this study there.

Making time for learning to learn in school

So important are these skills for learning in bottom strata schools that time should be allocated to it for some age groups at least, with planned reinforcement and practice across the school's formal knowledge domains and subjects. And teachers need the opportunity to acquire similar skills.

Teachers have an important role in coaching children in these skills, particularly when they are working in the contexts of their subjects. And so might staff such as learning mentors or personal advisers who might use certain alternative frameworks for developing children's greater competence in learning, such as the 'You Can Do It!' scheme based on research in Australia suggesting that an achievement orientation can be taught. Its materials are extensive. Another useful framework might use the domains of emotional intelligence described by Goleman (1996) to look at engagement in learning and wider contexts, thus aiding transfer.

Learning out of school

Children from middle class or advantaged homes enjoy many material and cultural resources throughout their years at school; they go to the theatre and other places of interest. They have space in which to do their homework and support in doing it. They have learning experiences and challenges outside school which develop their potential and resources, often in ways that make their learning strategies easily accessible in school.

Children in bottom strata schools need to be given similar learning advantages. They require the facility to undertake studies which complement those of mainstream activity, whether at an after-school club, in a community learning centre with internet access, or a chess or mathematics club where they can meet and learn with children from other schools and communities. They need access to the sporting, artistic and cultural activities available to middle class children and to learn in different contexts with their peers.

No school can provide all such opportunities, but all ought to be aware of and publicise what is available to pupils and parents. The opportunities to complement school programmes are available through voluntary organisations, the statutory and voluntary youth services, charities, businesses and, with the aid of outreach funds, orchestras, art galleries, museums and theatres. It is essential that parents and members of local organisations in the community are involved in planning and running activities, to avoid a contemporary equivalent of charity for the poor. Including parents and members of the local community allows their practical involvement in the mission of the school and, most importantly, begins to build bridges between formal and informal learning. This maximises the accessibility of all the children's learning strategies and cultural resources and begins to provide that context in which children can begin to see the transfer of their learning.

Making provision for non-learning needs

Many children bring social needs with them into school. They may be hungry or have housing problems, be involved in family or community conflict, or have violence on their minds. There are some things schools can do themselves. They can feed the children, as in the many breakfast and dinner clubs which have sprung up over the past few years. They can provide suitable clothing and ensure that the school dress may be purchased at modest rather than exclusive retailers.

With such needy children, schools have to be part of the networks of statutory and other services in their communities. The children's circumstances may first be noticed when they are in school so the school will often be the point of first referral. This has implications for the leadership in bottom strata schools, and for work on common agendas across the agencies for children, families and communities. The services themselves need to build on local funds of knowledge and respond to local needs.

Other learning needs

Also important to teaching and learning are the strategies normally expected of schools in challenging circumstances – work on improving attendance, behaviour, engagement, exclusions – the matters receiving most coverage in the media. Behaviour is certainly a major issue, particularly where resistance culture rules. Teachers need to be clear about how they deal with this recurrent background to their work, and may find the *relaxed vigilance* recommended by Rogers (2002) a useful approach. Behaviour management must be consistent across the school. School behaviour policies which are negotiated with children, parents and community are more likely to succeed, leading ultimately to children taking responsibility themselves. Self-talk (Rogers, 2000) and developing metacognition are internal personal mechanisms for support which can be learned.

Appropriate provision for dealing with challenging behaviour should also be made, whether in learning support units on site or by specialist support from outside. There are many sources of advice and support to schools, including universities, local education authorities and organisations in the voluntary and private sector. Many are the subject of national initiatives in the UK, with attached funding; many are quite new. But this book's concern is the learning disadvantage suffered by the children in bottom strata schools, which underpins not only their performance but whether they even turn up for lessons and how long they stay.

Providing a curriculum and pedagogy appropriate for bottom strata schools is a skilled, time-consuming and resource-intensive operation, particularly against the background of their context for learning and teaching. But if learning disadvantage is to be tackled, the resources must be provided and the time found. And even with the resources, there are implications for the leadership and capacity of the schools. These are considered in the next chapter.

Chapter 7
The development of learning schools and the implications for leadership

The development of learning schools

Chapter 6 argued that teaching needs to be a reflective activity, so as to respond to the daily complexity of trying to influence young minds. This complexity is compounded in bottom strata schools by the learning disadvantage of the pupils and their dissonance with the assumptions and cultures of schooling. Their teachers need to be especially open-minded about what is effective in classrooms, and be willing to go on learning. With the changing complexities of the communities the schools serve, the goal must be to develop as professional learning communities, or learning schools.

Staff

Schools striving for this goal will understand the importance of reflection for strengthening practice, and adopt a particular model as the basis for staff learning and development. This will need to incorporate productive processes for preparation and reflection, like the model developed by Senge *et al* (2000), reproduced in Figure 2.

Increasing and sharing knowledge about learning and teaching is an additional core purpose of the learning school and will be reflected in its policies. With the publication of national criteria for judging teaching (Ofsted, 1999b), more schools are developing teaching policies, often taking account of the specific pedagogies of the national literacy, numeracy and key stage 3 strategies. Policies that support teaching and learning appear to be a feature of effective schools (Gray *et al,* 1999) but must be firmly grounded in an understanding of children's learning.

In the learning school, all staff gatherings include a focus on learning and teaching. Teachers report back after training events, sharing reflections on their relevance for their school. They discuss work they are developing in their classrooms, possibly in groups. They share new strategies they have tried which appear successful with previously unresponsive children. Staff displays and newsletters reflect developing knowledge about learning and teaching and the involvement of all the staff. A member of the leadership team promotes, facilitates and supports staff learning as part of their agreed responsibilities. All the leadership team seek out success and reward it, ensuring good practice is promoted and networked.

Teachers expect to be learning continually and work with colleagues to improve their teaching, but they are not discouraged by being expected to achieve some unattainable notion of competence. New teachers see experienced colleagues continuing to learn and keeping an open mind about their effectiveness and what works in particular circumstances. All staff are encouraged to pursue personal learning objectives each year. One Bristol primary school published and displayed its staff's learning objectives at the main school entrance, so celebrating learning as the skilled process it is. As conscious learners, such teachers are helping develop their metacognition or 'meta-skills' (Stoll *et al,* 2003).

Professional development funding and non-contact time may at last be more available, thanks to *Time for Standards* (DfES, 2002c) and the 2003 agreement on workforce development. This could allow schools to discuss and implement the skills and agreements required for effective observation, as well as those for management monitoring. Part of school development budgets could be used to create a development entitlement for staff, to be spent however individuals choose for their own development. These entitlements might be pooled within a group and used by individuals or groups to pursue particular research. Outside training, particularly when expensive, will continue to be a delegate matter, as it is now in many schools, with staff attending courses about agreed priorities on behalf of the whole school.

A school that is a professional learning community is open to knowledge acquired from outside the school. It encourages staff to seek outside contacts and maintain professional networks with colleagues in other schools.

Pupils

The requirements to help children in bottom strata schools become self-confident and skilled learners were discussed in chapter 5. The way in which individual schools develop and implement appropriate measures will depend on their specific contexts for learning, which must be constantly re-evaluated. Schools need to consider whether there should be separate identified lessons in thinking skills; how the learning curriculum might underpin all teaching; how the skills, strategies and mental tools become prominent in all aspects of the school's work and the contacts between adults and children; how the overall expressive order of the school and its reward systems can reflect the importance of learning and the school's basic trust of the children. These decisions will not be taken once and for all but will be regularly reviewed as part of the learning process. The pupils need to be involved in this continuing exploration and empowered to ask searching questions of the staff and themselves. This learning process needs to be overseen by a member of the leadership team.

The learning curriculum will reflect national curriculum requirements (DfEE and QCA, 1999), and complement the move towards Individual Learning Plans by the age of 14 (DfES, 2002a), which are intended to help young people navigate their way through the 'new' 14-19 phase. This will particularly benefit those taking complicated routes post-14, possibly at more than one institution, and this is likely to include many students in bottom strata schools.

Parents and the community

Many community schools provide adult education on their premises, sometimes in conjunction with a further education college or community education service. This is a sensible use of the premises and equipment and can contribute more widely to the regeneration of an area. However, local needs should be thoroughly identified by the community and the agencies which serve it, not just by the school.

As schools develop as learning communities, they should enable parents to benefit from appropriate provision and help them support their children's learning. *Books for Babies*, for instance, is popular with parents of young children and the ensuing involvement in adult conversation aids the children's development. *Coping with Kids* enables parents of older children to learn together how to put effective boundaries round behaviour, and how these might change as their children grow. *Family learning*, supported by national funding, complements the national literacy and numeracy strategies. Here parents may learn alongside their children, sustaining both. For those from disadvantaged backgrounds, learning to be more effective parents and helping their children learn can be particularly empowering.

Provision of this kind is a gateway to further learning. In a group of schools in south Bristol, for example, parents took play supervision qualifications so that they could look after the children of other parents while they attended classes. A small number, facilitated by the community education service, took an access course for college in preparation for training as teachers. When they are back teaching in local schools, as they plan to do, the schools will have teachers who understand at first hand the nature of the children's learning disadvantage and who can tune into the children's language patterns and other community norms.

Some community groups run their own provision for children – community language classes, for example, or supplementary schools – which can complement and benefit school learning. Schools should have effective links with these local organisations, perhaps through the governors, and the schools' teachers and other staff should know what their pupils are learning there, so as to maximise the advantages for transfer. Training and support for teachers in community-run schools might be planned and organised collaboratively by the school and the organisations concerned.

The community needs to see the school as a place in which they are welcome. As well as adult classes, the routine meetings of community groups and tenants' associations, where learning is informal, can be held on school premises. Community newspapers might be produced using school facilities. If the local housing office or a first stop shop for other services is based in the school, the community will have access to many of the people they may wish to see. The concept of full service schools is discussed below.

Such practical use of school facilities helps build the funds of knowledge in the community into the life of the school. If school staff are involved with some of the activities involved, they will more readily understand the pupils' main ways of learning and modes of communication and their teaching will be more effective.

Links with the community and parents should be a responsibility of a member of the school leadership team, as these links strengthen classroom learning and study of the community has specific requirements. Expertise is needed in facilitating and observing groups, for example, and in writing up and interpreting conclusions for staff to incorporate in their practice and develop through their reflective cycles. Partnerships with universities or private or voluntary sector consultancies can be helpful, although they do require money and time.

Working with other schools

The staff of learning schools share knowledge and learning with each other, so encouraging teachers to be learners. This may be extended through nationally funded partnerships such as *Excellence in Cities* or *Education Action Zones* (DfEE, 1997a), or those set up by local initiatives to serve particular communities, such as local authority housing estates or entire cities or towns. Central government has expected greater collaboration between schools over the past few years (Blunkett, 2000b; DfES, 2002d) even though the education quasi-market persists. This is discussed in the next chapter.

In addition to the links made by schools and teachers for professional reasons, clusters or families of primary and secondary schools need to make links because of the families who have children at more than one school. Schools in urban areas are likely to be fairly near each other and could collaborate in their work with families and the community. Clusters can work together on the incorporation of funds of knowledge into the curriculum and on developing their understanding of the linguistic and other social conventions that draw pupils and older students successfully into learning. A cluster might be the appropriate forum in which to begin this work.

Potentially, clusters can be powerful in improving the educational provision made for the community by its schools. As Fullan (2001a) has shown, school change is more effective and more likely to be sustained across a wider district. Provided they are adequately re-sourced, partnerships across an area can do more than individual schools to give staff access to external knowledge and best practice. Wider learning communities can develop across specialisms or interest groups from different schools, allowing experimentation and reflection in subject areas, leadership, and in the practice of learning across a number of disciplines.

Schools and institutions further afield may contribute to the enrich-ment experiences which complement young people's learning in school. As part of their partnership role, specialist colleges may make provision for children who are gifted or talented, offer sporting opportunities across an area, or facilitate master classes for young (and old) musicians.

In each case, the headteachers, staff and governors involved can contribute to a wider vision for their communities, towns or cities. In many areas, this has been happening for years and the views of staff in local schools are welcomed on broader civic matters.

Working with other services

Working with community services and organisations is required by statute through the *Local Strategic Partnerships* required in the council areas receiving funding for the *Neighbourhood Renewal Strategy*. This government strategy is intended to bring about:

- ...lower worklessness; less crime; better health; better skills; and better housing and physical environment in all the poorest neigh-bourhoods; and

- to narrow the gap on these measures between the most deprived neighbourhoods and the rest of the country. (Social Exclusion Unit, 2001, p25)

In these 'most deprived neighbourhoods', the school will find itself working at local level with the police, social services, housing, health, and agencies such as education welfare. Historically, it has been difficult to ensure that agencies work together and share information, even from different departments of the same council – this is the fractured bureaucracy Whitty (2002) refers to. Different agencies have different targets and work to different national and statutory frameworks which are not always compatible, even when the government departments nationally do collaborate effectively. Referral routes are complex and may differ or overlap. Cross-referral between agencies in the communities served by bottom strata schools is often essential but can be difficult.

Voluntary sector projects that provide holiday activities, for example, or drug rehabilitation schemes, also exist in the neighbourhood, sometimes with funding from earlier projects or charities. Community centres may have some funding from the local council and provide a base for the projects. If overseen by community-generated steering groups or committees, these centres and projects have much greater potential than external professionals to make decisions about local priorities and exercise local leadership. In doing so, they provide another way of generating funds of knowledge which can enrich the school learning of the neighbourhood's children. The steering groups and their members can become key resources to the schools. The projects could also be studied by the pupils and outreach classrooms be located in the centres. The learning school will be on the lookout for such opportunities.

As learning schools work with this range of organisations, who is it who sees the whole child? The statutory and voluntary agencies will each have a little part of the picture; a large part will be possessed by the child, the family and the community. The complexity encountered in individual classrooms is not as great as the complexity of factors and personalities experienced in communities. So the agencies, like the schools, must keep open minds and be committed to learning and reflection on what works and what does not. Some of this reflection needs to be undertaken collaboratively. Just as the incorporation of funds of knowledge in the community is essential for bottom strata schools, so it is for these services.

The problem for all the agencies except schools is that parents and families often only see them when there has been trouble. This is not a good calling card. In addition, the long history of poor communication and uncoordinated action between professionals has left difficult legacies in some of the communities served by bottom strata schools, inhibiting dialogue. Public servants from many agencies will have had the experience (as I have) when taking a public meeting, of being blamed for a number of separate events perceived to be deliberately targeted at a particular community. These can be as diverse as the closure of a secondary, primary or special school, the racialised nature of school life, the cessation of late night bus services, the closure or removal of access to a day centre for elderly people, the ending of police patrols in a notorious shopping precinct, the closure of a community and/or adult education centre or the sale of a large redundant factory or playing field.

Collaboration between services is therefore essential; schools and agencies should jointly commit to learning and the incorporation of community funds of knowledge. As the difficulties children are experiencing may first be noticed or surmised at school and only then be drawn to the attention of relevant agencies, 'full-service' or even 'extended service' schools have been developed (Campbell and Whitty, 2002), where communities can access all the services they need in one location, and agencies are able to work more effectively with the children. This is one intention of the multi-agency *Sure Start* projects developed for very young children in the UK (DfEE, 2000), with overall direction coming from the community.

Initial evaluation of extended service schools suggests that the involvement of teachers with a wide range of agencies raises questions about the prime focus of their role. All the services need some adjustment and development (Campbell and Whitty, 2002) and such work seems a perfect opportunity for joint learning. On a more modest scale, police officers are based in some schools in the UK and some schools also have attached social workers, potentially making joint work with families easier.

Leadership and creation of capacity

In describing the development of bottom strata schools as professional learning communities, the responsibilities for at least four members of school leadership teams have been identified. In addition, effective collaboration on the scale described requires much management time, particularly when other agencies wish to meet a senior member of staff who can make agreements on behalf of the school. Learning is intensive for every one involved, in both personal and resource terms.

Added to the day to day context for working in these schools, described in chapter 4 – the huge and intense personal demands on staff, the frequent challenges to their authority and teaching skills, the variable emotional climate, the occasionally fraught relations with individual parents or families, and the schools' greater general vulnerability – a high priority for school leadership teams must be the creation of school capacity. Otherwise, the development of learning schools that explore and counter learning disadvantage will be difficult. Capacity involves the willingness to reflect; the organisational, professional and personal receptiveness to change; the indispensable energy and optimism; and the resources, time and skills.

Enrolling the staff in change

The staff too must be enrolled in the mission of the school. It starts with them; it largely falls on their shoulders; it is the staff who enrol the children, the parents and the community. In the past, too many headteachers and leadership teams have thought they could bring about change by themselves in spite of the staff. The Ofsted *Handbook for Inspection in England* (1999b) advises inspectors to consider whether 'there is a shared commitment to improvement and the capacity to succeed' in a school, when thinking about its leadership (p92 in the primary version, p86 in the secondary).

To bring about shared commitment, the leadership team must have a vision for the school, developed as the result of a process which has involved staff, governors, parents, the community and children. Visions can blind as well as enlighten (Fullan, 1993), and in learning schools and organisations, they have to be continually reviewed and examined even as they are being used. Visions will have changed by the time they are achieved, but they are important for making people think and can be powerful in providing a focus for action.

The leadership team is the steward or custodian of the school's vision (Senge, 1990). They interpret and re-interpret it for staff, clarifying the school goals and their role in achieving them, inspiring and motivating the staff as they do so. The leadership team is also a designer of learning processes for the staff (Senge, 1990). In the learning school, this involves supporting and developing the reflective processes with which this chapter began, focusing particularly on the exploration of learning disadvantage and the ways of countering it.

Holding up this vision, and developing learning in relation to it, helps staff find the meaning in their work that is fundamental to effective change and development (Fullan, 2001a). The professional narratives staff develop alone and with their colleagues provide a framework for this meaning and for their sense of the significance of what they do and how coherent it is (see chapter 2). This affects their enthusiasm and their commitment: the leadership team's task is to help staff in their meaning making and in creating coherence in the school's work (Fullan, 2001b).

Learning takes time. For teachers in learning schools, this means resisting pressure and allowing a sensible pace for change, so that the result is fundamental and long-lasting, not just an alternative set of learning drills for children, with no clearer purpose or underlying principles.

Fullan (2001a) notes three levels of classroom change. At one level, there is the introduction of new materials, possibly to supplement an existing teaching approach. At the next, there is the introduction of new strategies or activities, such as the literacy hour or daily mathematics lesson in the UK, which have certainly changed the way teaching is approached (Earl *et al*, 2003). Most fundamental, however, is the change in teachers' beliefs, understandings and theories about teaching. To succeed in bringing about real change, appropriate to the circumstances of class and school, this third level must be achieved. It is at this level that drills cease to be drills and the purposes and meanings of change are understood. This enables teachers to modify and adapt what they are doing to suit the specific combinations of young minds they encounter on the basis of knowledge. This is a slow and uneven process but a necessary goal of the learning school.

Undertaking continuous learning in such a way is challenging and the leadership team must try to reduce and make manageable the external pressures on staff. In Hopkins' view (2001), effective schools are those which focus on whatever is important at the time to the achievement of their goals, resisting outside pressures to do otherwise or, if necessary, incorporating such pressures into their own priorities and using them for the contribution they can make.

It is far easier to do this from the secure position of a high-achieving school serving an advantaged community, with reliable attainment and good inspection reports. Many bottom strata schools, by contrast, when under pressure from external agencies as well as their day to day demands, are tempted to look to the short term and fulfil as many of the exogenous requirements as possible. But although these short term fixes may reduce pressure temporarily, they will not guarantee long term success (Hopkins, 2001; Tribal Education, 2002) unless geared to an articulated vision and the processes of institutional learning described. Managing this is important for city schools to be successful (Ofsted, 2000b).

An important related aspect of the leadership team's role is helping to manage the impact on staff of the school's day to day demands. Staff need to know they have support in dealing with all dimensions of classroom life, whether through the development of more effective pedagogy, dealing with challenging behaviour, or meeting distressed parents. Whether they feel supported or not in this way is a good indicator of staff relations.

Mechanisms for building capacity

Exercising leadership in the ways discussed here helps create capacity for the staff in bottom strata schools. Other management mechanisms, such as the creation of a 'cadre' of staff (Hopkins, 2001) can also help bring about change. This model, together with recommendations for a phased change programme, are included in the DfEE handbook for the *Schools Facing Challenging Circumstances* scheme (Hopkins *et al*, 2001) (see chapter 2).

The cadre is a group of staff interested in introducing change in their own classrooms who are given the time to try out different approaches to teaching and learning. They then help colleagues think about and introduce similar changes on a phased basis. The advantage is that some of the consequences of these changes have already been considered and worked through. The cadre is a cross-hierarchical group of interested staff, with a variety of experiences and subject or age backgrounds, not the school's leadership team. The cadre concept derives from the continuing IQEA (Improving the Quality of Education for All) project and rests on the belief that time-consuming development work needs to be broadly based and routed through a group separate from the school's leadership team, but empowered by it and given the capacity to do the work. As the National College for School Leadership (NCSL, 2002a) observe, there is a need to separate 'the generation of capacity from how it is used' (p6).

The attraction of this model is that it begins with interest, enthusiasm and commitment and, although it needs to be supported and resourced by the school's leadership team, it is not management driven, top down determined change. It creates capacity outside the leadership team and involves more staff in leadership roles. Teachers are also more likely to listen seriously to their colleagues about the introduction of change in classrooms than to those in positions of responsibility or from outside the school (Huberman, 1983). The leadership team can keep itself at maximum capacity and has enlisted a group of staff to do some of the school's thinking for it. Both groups are engaged in the reculturing necessary for a learning organisation (Fullan, 1993).

This is just one model. Schools must seek their own mechanisms for learning and developing their capacity. The key features of the IQEA approach – engaging enthusiasm and spreading learning throughout the staff – are certainly worth considering. Given the need to keep the school improvement plan simple (Stoll and Fink, 1995), there could be more than one of these teams operating at once, depending on the breadth of the focus needed. Teams could also include other stakeholders.

Leadership in bottom strata schools
The components and tasks of leadership
Some of the key components of leadership have already been dis-cussed – being custodians of the school's vision, developing learning

systems, helping staff develop meaning in the work they are engaged in, creating capacity, helping create coherence, choosing the priorities for the school which further its goals and, in the learning school, developing an organisation suffused with reflective processes and the time to make effective change. Leadership teams generally work on enrolling staff and building a joint commitment or, in Ofsted's (1999b) words:

> ... creating and securing commitment to a clear vision; managing change so as to improve the school; building a high-performing team; inspiring, motivating and influencing staff; leading by example. (p96)

Fullan (2001b) defines the key components of leadership as *coherence making, knowledge creation and sharing*, working on *relationships, understanding the change process* and *moral purpose*. Coherence making arises from the need for everyone involved to draw meaning from change, since there is danger of fragmentation in a complex organisation such as a school. *Knowledge creation and sharing* is the purpose of the learning school, as its reflective basis develops and improves in relation to the study of learning disadvantage. Unless *relationships* are a constant focus of the leadership team, it is impossible to enrol the staff – or the children, parents or community. The team must also invest in *understanding the change process* if they are to encourage development and explain its significance for staff. Fullan's final component, *moral purpose* is essentially why teachers enter the profession in the first place (Fullan, 1993); the purpose for those leading the school is to realise their belief in the worth of what the school is doing to combat learning disadvantage and in the school's ability to do so. No single component is appropriate all the time.

These five components of leadership are closely connected and the leadership team needs to be active in all of them. Only thus will the messy process of effective change move in the right direction, and staff and stakeholders understand what needs to be done. The leadership team need also to maintain and develop the school's operational systems to serve the school's mission appropriately: recruitment and induction of staff, overall planning, assessment of children with special educational needs, guidance systems for children (and staff), keeping premises healthy and safe and ensuring parents are responded to appropriately. Careful performance monitoring and evaluation should operate at all levels of the school. The leadership team will also work on effective partnership arrangements and the maintenance of good relationships with neighbours and the community.

Unlike in business, members of the leadership team are also part of the school's operational systems. They often deal with children and parents directly and, in the context of bottom strata schools especially, ensure their schools remain generally calm by being visible and accessible around the buildings and site (Ofsted, 2000b).

Leading learners

How leadership is exercised in a learning organisation will influence how the school's vision is achieved. The notions and theories that have been developed about the practical exercise of leadership can inspire those who lead and can make them think, but what matters is their applicability in specific contexts.

Invitational leadership (Stoll and Fink, 1995; Stoll *et al*, 2003) invites staff and stakeholders to participate in the development and fulfilment of the vision for a school. *Instructional* leadership (Hopkins, 2001) ensures the focus of school improvement is on teaching and what Hopkins describes as 'powerful learning'. *Distributive* leadership is being advanced through the National College for School Leadership in the UK (NCSL, 2002b) and suggests that leadership should be exercised by a wide group of staff if it is to be effective. Leadership may also be defined as *transformational* or *inclusive*, and may embrace several of these models at once.

Goleman (2000) has developed a typology of leadership styles – coercive, authoritative, affiliative, democratic, pacesetting and coaching. He found that leaders often used different styles at different times, depending on circumstance and the state of development of their organisations, and that coercive and pacesetting styles of leadership negatively affected both climate and performance.

Leadership teams must decide for themselves, as part of their own learning and development as a team, which of these models or styles, or combinations of both, are appropriate for their circumstances at a particular time. School leadership teams are also leading other groups of learners – adults and children. The development of the learning school is an exploration in complex circumstances, particularly in bottom strata schools because of the nature of learning disadvantage and the diversity in their contexts and communities. Just as teachers must be expected to keep an open mind about the effects of what they do and commit themselves to learning as the way to guarantee improvement, so it is with leaders. Leadership teams therefore need to be leading learners in both senses of the phrase.

Like the rest of the staff, the leadership team will be studying the community and its children so as to draw them more effectively into learning. As they do this, they will reflect on the implications for their leadership and the effects on the school of their actions. It is in this context that they consider and learn about aspects and models of leadership and their relevance to the circumstances and tasks in hand. As Fullan (2001b) observes:

> (there) can never be a recipe or cookbook for change, nor a step-by-step process. Even sophisticated plans (published in management textbooks) ... are suspect if used as the basis for planning. They may be useful to stir one's thinking... (p44/45).

This is true of all aspects of change: in the face of complexity leaders also need to be learners. What applies to all learners applies to them – the need for reflective cycles, the need to model their learning for others, the need to develop their skills, the need for access to external knowledge and the need for some time, often away from the school, to mull things over and allow slow thinking. Leadership teams receive pressure in the form of professional expectation from their own staff but also from the expectations of their wider learning community. With the pressure of maintaining a bottom strata school day by day, pressure may be needed to ensure that leadership learning goes on. This is potentially one of the most important functions of local education authorities in the UK. As part of the 'wider-district' (Fullan, 2001a), the generation of a climate of high expectation and support is essential in urban schools, and more difficult for central government to sustain in an inclusive way.

Who exercises leadership in the learning school?

Any school, like any organisation, needs a team which regularly oversees the whole of the school's activity and whose members have strategic responsibilities for staff learning, children's learning, links with parents and the community and other cross-school areas, to ensure that the work progresses and is of the appropriate standard. Where significant areas of development are required across school activity, they need champions with the authority to ensure that these developments do take place.

The teams can be quite small: head plus deputy, or they can include assistant heads, bursars and finance officers. With discrete time for meetings, and the greater distance developed between 'management' and classroom teachers because of the quasi-market (Ball, 1994), a team of this kind in secondary schools can seem rather remote to the classroom teacher. At its worst, this will inhibit teachers' sense of ownership of any school-wide vision, ethos or direction.

To counteract this, not only must the leadership team be accessible but as many staff as possible must be involved in leadership developments (NCSL, 2002b) and prepared for wider roles or promotion. This offers a fresh perspective on return to the classroom, as many who have undertaken secondments will testify; problems are approached from a different direction. Leadership is demystified and the expertise and understanding of the whole staff is better harnessed to contribute to effective development.

Ofsted (1999b) refers to 'the headteacher and key staff' (p92), who are expected to exercise responsibility for leadership and management in a school. Although there is always a visible small team, a much wider group of staff – and other key stakeholders at times who bring a different perspective – need to be involved. In bottom strata schools, the active involvement of members of the community in some aspects of leadership can contribute to their empowerment through learning and their enrolment into the mission of the school. And the skills of the leadership team are extended. This is inclusive leadership.

The dangers of pathologising leadership

This is not necessarily the traditional view in the English-speaking world, or indeed in some of the current national narratives:

> Our traditional views of leaders – as special people who set the direction, make the key decisions and energise the troops – are deeply rooted in an individualistic and non-systemic worldview ... (our) traditional view of leadership is based on assumptions of people's powerlessness, their lack of personal vision and inability to master the forces of change, deficits which can only be remedied by a few great leaders. (Senge, 1990, p340)

The role of the headteacher or principal has been rightly identified as central for 'successful schools' (National Commission on Education, 1993; Teddlie and Stringfield, 1993; Ofsted, 2002b) and effective national change (Ofsted, 2000a; Earl *et al,* 2003). To work effectively on the components of leadership described above, an effective team must be built round the headteacher.

But with the cultural assumptions described by Senge in media images, popular profiles of effective leaders and the focus on the personal in many public narratives in all walks of life, the leadership role is in danger of being pathologised. Stoll and Myers (1998) point out that much early writing about school failure was about management rather than what happened in the classroom; thus was born the notion of the 'superhead' to 'turn round' these schools. Public comments were made about the failures of headteachers in connection with the failure to achieve the national literacy and numeracy targets in the UK in 2002. And the guidance associated with the *Leadership Incentive Grant* (DfES, 2002d), available to a restricted number of schools, many of them in the bottom strata, focused strongly on the removal of ineffective leaders, as did a widely publicised email to local education authorities.

In a challenging bottom strata school going through a difficult stage, for example when leadership has been criticised or removed after an inspection, the staff can feel powerless, believing the locus of control does not rest with them, and that they are not responsible because it was the leadership that was poor. Assumptions by stakeholders such as parents at a time like this about the inherent worthlessness of the staff, analogous to the harmful notions of fixed ability, can continue to damage the school and make improvement even more difficult.

Such pathologisation also gives the opportunity to those whose job it is to encourage and support the school – the governing body or local education authority – to evade their responsibilities. Mix this together with a strong dose of the crisis narrative, and there is a potent formula for faltering development or recurrent failure.

The removal of leadership is entirely appropriate in certain circumstances, though it must be done with dignity. But leadership alone is not responsible for improving attainment in schools, when change is so complex, the context problematic and contributions are required from all staff. Effective leaders are certainly vital. And heroes do exist – they energise organisations, including schools, to improve themselves. But this is never the whole story and the dependence on heroes is not a satisfactory way to run a system, as Senge points out. Everyone has responsibility. New leadership in a school begins by building the capacity of the staff and establishing positive relationships with stakeholders. Leadership and leading learners is a shared activity.

Study of the role of leadership and management in relation to national strategies is a productive contribution to knowledge and change. But it must not be the only or even the main focus lest it demonise the staff who might be making significant contributions to the children's learning and well-being. The pathologisation of leadership is the obverse side of the crisis narrative coin.

Future possibilities

Much is now understood about how to combat learning disadvantage in bottom strata schools. But how feasible and how likely is it that the complex procedures required will be set in motion? To answer this question, we need to look at the national framework for the work of schools operating in the UK today.

Chapter 8
Government policy in the UK and the work of bottom strata schools

The national framework for schools in the UK

This chapter focuses on the aspects of the national framework for compulsory schooling in the UK that are directly relevant to the learning, teaching and school leadership matters explored in the last three chapters. What room for manoeuvre does the framework permit schools for countering learning disadvantage or establishing a climate in which to foster learning?

We saw how one aspect of the national framework, the quasi-market, has concentrated the effects of learning disadvantage by creating bottom strata schools in urban areas in the first place. Alongside this are the measures intended to raise standards overall; the national literacy and numeracy strategies that have driven primary school reform for over five years; the measures intended to transform secondary education; and the additional provision made for schools in urban areas. This chapter examines these measures in the context of the quasi-market, and concludes with a review of recent government publications which may promise some changes, such as the documents on the national strategies for primary and secondary schools.

Raising standards

Current measures to raise attainment in English schools have been unfolding since 1989. Characterised in *Schools - Building on Suc-*

cess (DfEE, 2001) as 'high challenge, high support' (p9), the measures are intended to work like this:

1. Standards are set by the national curriculum, which provides guidance for what needs to be taught in schools.

2. Schools assume responsibility for raising their standards, aided by the increasing levels of funding delegated to them under their control, with schools in urban areas receiving significantly enhanced funding in recognition of the 'greater challenges they face'.

3. Schools set targets for improving their performance on the basis of comparative data provided by Ofsted and local education authorities.

4. Schools consider the best ways of achieving their targets, taking information on best practice from a variety of sources, including websites constructed for the purpose. They send their staff on training and professional development courses, which are now available to an unprecedented degree.

5. Schools are held to public account by Ofsted inspection and by the publication of performance tables.

6. Relatively unsuccessful schools are inspected more frequently to help them improve. More successful ones are inspected less often and given greater freedoms through the principle of *earned autonomy*.

7. Intervention in schools takes place when appropriate and in *inverse proportion to success*. This is largely the responsibility of local education authorities, which are also expected to support schools and challenge them to do better. Their work is governed by a *Code of Practice* (DfEE, 1998b).

Target setting became an important national process in 1998. Schools set their targets with an eye to the achievement of 'similar' schools – those with comparable percentages of children entitled to free school meals or speaking English as an Additional Language. School targets were also intended to contribute to those of their local education authority, which in turn contributed to national targets. National 2002 targets for eleven year olds (key stage 2) in English and Mathematics were announced soon after Labour came to power in 1997, but actually reflected a Conservative manifesto promise (Conservative Party, 1997).

Following the publication of the green paper *Teachers – meeting the challenge of change* (DfEE, 1998d), formal internal school accountability for standards was added, along with performance management for teaching staff. Annual objectives were agreed with teachers for the first time in 2001 and their progression up the pay spine is now regulated. Teachers can pass through a 'performance threshold' after a nationally-moderated formal assessment, earning a further salary increase. Headteachers' objectives, reviewed in relation to their salaries, are set by their governing bodies and must make reference to pupil performance. These measures were the beginnings of what has become known as 'workforce remodelling' (DfES, 2002c), considered later in this chapter.

The regulatory framework of the national curriculum which largely governed what was to be taught was supplemented by the introduction into primary schools of the national literacy and numeracy strategies. Although not compulsory, aspects of the strategies were included in the Ofsted Inspection Handbook (1999b). The strategies provided detailed prescriptions for the processes of teaching, that is how the curriculum was to be taught, and became the central thrust of primary school reform directed at achieving the 2002 national targets. Although now subsumed into the wider primary strategy (DfES, 2003b), they are still in place.

The national literacy and numeracy strategies

The national literacy and numeracy strategies were introduced in 1998 and 1999 respectively into all English primary schools, following national pilot projects run under the Conservative government and the publication of national task group reports (DfEE, 1997b, 1998c). The task group for literacy was appointed while Labour was in opposition and that for numeracy soon after it came to power.

The national literacy strategy's *Framework for Teaching* (DfEE, 1998e) indicates the level of detail involved in the prescription. It describes the features of successful teaching (discursive, interactive, well-paced, confident and ambitious – p8) and the strategies to be employed (direction, demonstration, modelling, scaffolding, explanation, questioning, exploration, investigation of ideas, discussion and argument, listening and responding). The features and strategies are then related to the structure of the literacy hour.

The literacy hour was to begin with about 15 minutes on whole class shared text work (reading from a text, choosing a focus for comprehension, or composing texts), followed by 15 minutes whole class word or sentence work (phonics, spelling and vocabulary) and up to 20 minutes guided writing or reading for half the class and independent work for the other half. The teacher was expected to work with two ability groups a day while the rest of the children worked by themselves. The literacy hour was to conclude with a plenary, to be a summary of the main teaching points by teachers and children, and practice of what had been learned.

The national numeracy strategy (DfEE, 1999b) outlined a similar lesson structure, beginning with oral work and mental calculation, continuing with the main teaching activity (teacher input and pupil activities) and concluding with a plenary. But it did not require the full hour until towards the end of Key Stage 2. As for literacy, particular teaching strategies were recommended.

This detailed prescription was accompanied by the publication of extensive materials, a large scale training programme available to all schools and the appointment of national strategy teams, each with regional directors. Local education authorities appointed their own literacy and numeracy consultants and provided intensive support for primary schools with the lowest performance, as measured by their previous results. As implementation proceeded, elements of the strategies continued to be modified in the light of emerging issues and problems (Earl et al, 2003) and extra training was provided for teachers. Additions were made to the strategies, such as 'Wave 2' provision for small groups of children considered to be at risk of slow progress, and 'Wave 3' for children who needed one-to-one support. There were booster classes and the Additional Literacy Strategy; materials were produced for children with special educational needs and those for whom English is an additional language.

The national targets for eleven year olds were expressed in terms of the percentage of children to achieve the Level 4 benchmark. For

2002 these were set at 80 per cent for English and 75 per cent for Mathematics. Targets for 2004 of 85 per cent for both subjects were announced in 2001, involving further local education authority targets. These were calculated by the application of a statistical matrix to the published results in 2000 and in practice meant that the lower attaining LEAs and their schools had to make the biggest improvements.

Outcomes and the implications for bottom strata schools

Although the government appeared buoyed by the rising performance of eleven year olds when it announced the extension of the primary literacy and numeracy strategies into secondary schools (Blunkett, 2000b), the 2002 targets were not achieved. The English results stalled in 2001 and remained at the same level in the following year. Those for Mathematics dropped in 2001, but then rose. The upshot was that in 2002 achievement was 75 per cent in English and 73 per cent in Mathematics. Much public speculation followed on whether the results for English and Mathematics could rise any further in primary schools and if so, how. After consultation, the government published what it intended to do (DfES, 2003b).

So what had happened and what is the significance for the future success of education reform? A great deal has been written about the national strategies, much of it positive but much of it critical because of the extent of the prescription and the emphasis on performance outcomes. In a contested field, the official evaluation is drawn on here, commissioned by the government from the Ontario Institute for Studies in Education (OISE) because of its broad focus.

The evaluation produced three reports, culminating with *Watching and Learning 3* (Earl *et al*, 2003). It was extensive, based on semi-structured interviews; postal surveys; observation of meetings, training sessions and lessons; visits to schools; a review of the relevant research; and an analysis of the documentation. The evaluation was undertaken from the perspective of large-scale reform, one of the particular interests and areas of expertise of the OISE team (which included Michael Fullan), but it also examined the implications for teachers and schools of initiating such a detailed strategy.

The OISE evaluation found that the strategies had changed the nature of primary education in England. The teaching frameworks largely adopted, teaching was now based more on learning objectives than activities, and teachers demonstrated awareness of the different levels of understanding of each of their pupils (p3). This enabled them to set curriculum targets for individual pupils and these had become much more 'salient' (p5). The gains arising from the strategies are in accordance with the research on good learning considered in chapter 5 of this book.

'Regional directors, (local education authority) consultants, headteachers and teachers' all thought that pupils' learning had been improved by the improved teaching (p3) and, even though the national targets had not been achieved, the rises in measured attainment had been substantial.

The OISE team also praised the strength of the national infrastructure, leading down from the national directors through the regional directors and local education authority consultants to the schools, where it had enabled capacity to develop. OISE said that many schools are 'becoming learning communities, working collaboratively, making decisions jointly, and taking more collective responsibility for school self-evaluation' (p5). These are positive developments for teacher learning and school change (see chapter 6).

But the OISE team also found that much remained to be done. Most of the improvement in attainment seemed to have occurred before the introduction of the strategies and some headteachers and teachers expressed doubt to the team about their importance. They were not alone; Tymms and Fitz-Gibbon (2001) question 'aspects of (the) validity and accuracy' (p171) of the reported rise in attainment. Their view is that there have been gains in Mathematics but not in English.

Many teachers still needed to know more about the teaching of literacy and mathematics; few had had the 'sustained learning experiences necessary to develop a thorough understanding' of the strategies (p6). Even more worrying, many teachers believed that the 'job was done'. These teachers had not reached Fullan's third level of change (see chapter 7), where the pedagogical principles behind the strategies are understood. Only at this level do teachers have the capacity to make informed adaptations to the strategies' materials and approaches, reflecting the starting points for their pupils' learning. Unless curriculum and pedagogy are attuned to the pupils, their learning may be compromised, aspirations impaired and their learning disadvantage possibly as severe as ever. If the third level of change is not reached, the introduction of changes in classrooms could remain mechanical rather than reflective. Schools need to have (or develop) the capacity to enable all their teachers to reach Fullan's third level of change.

The OISE report also noted that the high profile national targets and the high stakes accountability systems had had unintended effects, such as narrowing the curriculum in some schools and burdening teachers and children with 'considerable test preparation' (p7). Massive external pressure on schools to implement change carried the danger that a 'culture of dependence' might develop, 'reducing professional autonomy' (p6). This would make it more difficult to develop the capacity required to embed the reforms at a deeper level. The OISE team were told about concerns over initiative overload and the difficulties in some schools of maintaining the focus on key priorities, making further development difficult.

These findings raise important considerations for all schools, but particularly for those in the bottom strata. The OISE report pointed up some specific needs of schools serving disadvantaged communities. They reported:

> ...particular difficulties, perhaps related to some parents' own ambivalence towards school, their lack of conviction that education will improve their children's lives, and the overwhelming pressures many families in those communities face. (p8)

The evaluation team felt that '...to close the gap between high and low performing children ...... may require more attention to out-of-school influences on pupil attainment'.

Earl *et al* counsel against any further high profile target setting. They recognised the need for reduced central pressure and school capacity building so the changes could be deepened in all schools. This book has made a similar case. And, like this book, OISE stated that engagement with parents and consideration of the children's starting points for learning – their material, cultural and linguistic resources – are vital for bottom strata schools.

Two other issues are worth mentioning.

1 Pedagogy and Learning

One is the nature of the pedagogies prescribed by the strategies and the criticism made that they were limiting on teachers. Reynolds (1998), who was chair of the national numeracy task force and nationally influential, says in a review of the research on teaching and learning that:

> ...children learn more in classes where they spend more time being taught or supervised by their teacher than working on their own ... (and) ... teacher-led discussion as opposed to individual work dominates.... The effective teacher carries the content personally to the student, rather than relying on curriculum material or textbooks to do so... (but) this should not be equated with a traditional 'lecturing and drill' approach in which the students remain passive. Active teachers ask a lot of questions ... and involve students in class discussion ... students are kept involved in the lesson and the teacher has a chance to monitor children's understanding of the concepts taught. (p149/150)

Reynolds' observations support some of the descriptions of successful teaching in the national literacy strategy (DfEE, 1998e) while not insisting on a particular time schedule. He echoes the view of reflective pedagogy discussed in chapter 6 and what he says is consistent with the need to provide learning experiences of different shapes, types and durations, provided the teacher is clear about children's understanding and conceptual development and is actively involving them in the learning process. Unless teaching is as Reynolds describes, it is difficult to achieve such clarity. It is important that teachers vary the way they organise the time they spend with children because of the varied pace of learning. If the whole curriculum were taught on the basis of equal slots organised according to the clock, pupils' learning would be impaired.

2 Capacity-building

Capacity-building, identified in chapter 7 as so vital for bottom strata schools, is also considered by OISE. They found that capacity building was significantly enhanced by the national strategies' infrastructure, allowing teachers in all schools to learn from knowledge and practice elsewhere and the schools requiring the greatest support to receive it.

It needs to be emphasised in the training of regional directors and local education authority consultants, however, that the variation in children's starting points for learning is key to the teaching process. Otherwise, the reforms could remain mechanical and the greater flexibility advised by Earl *et al* will not become a reality.

Transforming secondary education

If primary education was the Labour government's priority in its first term, secondary was to follow in the next. A programme to transform secondary education was announced in a speech to a North of England Conference (Blunkett, 2000a), developed by the green paper and white paper on either side of the 2001 election (DfEE, 2001; DfES, 2001) and enacted in the 2002 Education Act. The secondary reform programme has the following features:

*   *The Key Stage 3 Strategy* – this was the development of the primary literacy and numeracy strategies for secondary school use, with appropriate pedagogy and training programme. Although the pedagogy is based on an input, practice-under-supervision and recap model, it has greater flexibility than for primary schools: starting activities can be considered for a number of lessons and the variability in the length of lessons between schools is recognised. The strategy came complete with targets, a national infrastructure similar to the primary, summer schools and catch-up materials. From the start, however, it was wider than the primary strategies. It was intended to cover Science and ICT (with far less prescription), and to affect teaching and learning in all subjects. Young people could now complete key stage 3 a year early, at the age of 13, if appropriate.

*   The *Schools Facing Challenging Circumstances* programme – this has been complemented by a *Leadership Incentive Grant* available to secondary schools which qualify for the scheme, plus those with more than 35 per cent of their students eligible for free school meals, those in Education Action Zones and those in areas covered by the various manifestations of *Excellence in Cities* (DfES, 2002d).

- *The development of City Academies* – these are intended to replace 'seriously failing schools' in deprived areas (Blunkett, 2000a, p20). Academies, as they are now more simply termed, are built and managed by partnerships of government, voluntary, church and business sponsors. In return for finding up to 20 per cent of the capital costs, the sponsors are represented on the board of trustees which replaces the governing body. The schools cease to be maintained by their local education authority and are funded nationally, direct from the DfES, although the local education authority can nominate trustees. In effect, they are state-funded independent schools. The first three opened in 2002.

- An *Academy for Gifted and Talented Youth* – this is to help develop national provision. It ran its first summer school in 2002 for 100 children, selected by test, but experienced recruitment problems for 2003.

- The *diversity agenda* or *diversity framework* (Morris, 2002b) – this is the increased specialisation of secondary schools, intended eventually to be extended to all of them (DfES, 2003a). The designations available to secondary schools are:

  - *Academies*

  - *Faith schools*, expected to expand in number, building on the aspirations of the Church of England (Church of England, 2001) and other faiths

  - schools in the *Leading Edge Programme*, open to high-performing specialist schools after five years

  - *beacon schools*, identified mainly by Ofsted and funded to share good practice (although this status is to be replaced by the Leading Edge Programme)

  - *training schools*, which are partners in schemes for initial teacher training and responsible for disseminating good practice

  - *specialist schools* in technology, sports, arts, languages, business and enterprise, engineering, maths and science, humanities, music and those with a 'rural' emphasis (DfES,

2003a). They can select a proportion of their intake and since 1997 have had to demonstrate the contribution they make to their local family of schools.

Other schools can be 'working towards' specialist status or run under contract by private sector or other organisations. By September 2003, 1200 schools were designated as specialists (DfES, 2003a).

• *a new unified phase for 14-19* – this is to be developed over several years (DfES, 2002a). Young people are now to have an individual learning plan to plot their pathways post-14. A different pattern of qualifications is to be introduced – possibly including an English baccalaureate – and the core curriculum modified. To overcome barriers to learning, students have access to the *Connexions* Service, established after the publication of a Social Exclusion Unit report (1999).

Pathfinders for diversity and 14-19 were funded and encouraged by the government, and contrary to the pressures of the quasi-market, all required a deliberate focus on collaboration. Tim Brighouse's (2002) notion of 'collegiates' was explored in the context of one such pathfinder and government acknowledged that a unified 14-19 phase would not be possible for many young people without effective collaboration between secondary schools and further education colleges. Similarly, *federations* of schools, with one headteacher, continue to be explored by the government through its reform of school governance, and as one possible response to weak leadership (DfES, 2002d).

Excellence in Cities and the London Challenge
Two major initiatives have been targeted at urban schools, namely Excellence in Cities and the London Challenge. *Excellence in Cities* was launched in March 1999 (DfEE, 1999a) and made available in inner London; Manchester and Salford; Liverpool and Knowsley; Birmingham; Leeds and Bradford; and in Sheffield and Rotherham. In 2000, it was extended to a further 21 local education authorities, although without funding for primary schools. The following year it was extended again, both as a full programme and in clusters, whereby schools and authorities in smaller urban areas could bid for a restricted number of the programme's components.

Excellence in Cities is a big programme, the first specifically to be targeted at urban areas; the earlier Education Action Zones dealt with deprivation but were not restricted to urban areas. The programme has four 'core beliefs' of

- high expectations on every individual;
- diversity;
- networks; and
- extending opportunity.

These echo other aspects of national policy and are intended to be at the heart of the programme's six strands, all of which are compulsory (except in the clusters) and highly prescriptive. They are:

- *Gifted and Talented* – each school identifies a cohort of between five and 10 per cent of its children using national criteria for participation in a programme of appropriate activities. These are available in-class and as enrichment, sometimes organised by other schools. This strand is seen as key to combating the 'wasted talent and disappointed ... families who aspire for their children to succeed' (DfEE, 1999a, p4).

- *Learning Mentors and Learning Support Units* – learning mentors are employed by schools with job descriptions similar to those of the personal advisers employed by *Connexions*. From a variety of professional backgrounds, they work on a time-limited basis with individual young people to help overcome their barriers to learning, in school or out. Learning Support Units do the same for young people with challenging behaviour and all secondary schools in Excellence in Cities areas are expected to have access to one. The Units are designed to ensure that the education of other students is not disrupted.

- *City Learning Centres (CLCs)* – these are state-of-the-art Information and Communications Technology centres, accessible to the community and partner primaries and operating on behalf of the whole Excellence in Cities partnership (see below). They provide intense experiences for students and staff, and create excellent curriculum materials and resources.

- *Beacon schools* – quotas of schools qualifying under the national criteria were agreed for each Excellence in Cities partnership.

- *Specialist Schools* – here, quotas were agreed, with schools meeting the national standards automatically receiving specialist status.

- *Small Education Action Zones* (or Excellence in Cities Action Zones) – this status is applied for by clusters of around a dozen schools, rather than the 20+ required for earlier zones. The cluster develops an action plan to raise the attainment of children at all key stages based on its allocation of funding. Unlike the earlier zones, the small ones are not separate legal identities and are not premised on exclusion of the local education authority. Nor is the influence of business on the curriculum a key design feature. They also receive less money and are expected to undertake fewer activities.

Excellence in Cities partnerships may also be allowed funding from the *Excellence Challenge* scheme, allocated for students from year 9 upwards to universities on the one hand, and schools and colleges on the other. The scheme is intended to raise aspirations in connection with higher education among young people in deprived areas and contribute to the government's 2010 target of 50 per cent participation by the age of 30.

In July 2002, the Secretary of State added the London Challenge as a further initiative (Morris, 2002b). The challenge was described as the comparatively low performance of secondary schools in London, the steep stratification of schools (and the associated high numbers of children attending independent schools), the expressed dissatisfaction of employers with the skills of students leaving state schools, and the difficulty of planning effectively across a large number of small London boroughs whose LEAs are of variable quality.

The programme that emerged for the London Challenge included tailor-made improvement plans for poorly performing schools, greater freedom for strong headteachers and the removal of weak ones, 30 more Academies and 'at least' 290 specialist schools. There was to be a new London Gifted and Talented Centre and a programme to ensure that every school was backed by business. A mortgage guarantee was to be available to teachers and two new forms of special status – Chartered London Teacher Status and London Commissioner Status – were to reflect the importance of teaching in the capital. All forms of indiscipline in schools were to receive a 'relentless focus'. Strategic leadership for the challenge was to be provided by having a minister responsible for it and a London Schools Commissioner to work across the boroughs. Tim Brighouse took up this post in January 2003.

Diversity, collaboration and the future of the comprehensive principle

Diversity has been a theme in UK education policy for over a decade. The DfE white paper (1992) *Choice and Diversity* argued that 'Uniformity in educational provision presupposes that children are all basically the same and that local communities have essentially the same educational needs' (p3.) And on page 9, it states: 'Diversity and parental choice allow schools to develop in different ways. In particular, they encourage schools to play to their strengths'.

Schools – Building on Success (DfEE, 2001) similarly extolled the benefits of 'greater diversity of provision', but also said this about the role of specialist schools:

> ... every school should have the opportunity and responsibility to make a contribution to a family of schools, to the development of the system as a whole or to the local community. (p47)

The specialist secondary schools system that the government (DfES, 2003a) is aiming to establish is thus to be based not just on diversity but also on collaboration. Schools are to make a contribution beyond their gates. Barber (2000a) is illuminating when he combines these strands to explain how the government is thinking:

> .... we require modernised comprehensive schools which meet the aspirations of all children whether they have special needs or have extraordinary talent. We need schools which focus on individuals, challenge them always to do better, set them ambitious, achievable targets, remove barriers to learning wherever necessary and link them to opportunities in other schools, in the community and in out-of-school places of learning. No pupil's education should be confined or restricted simply because of the school they happen to attend. (p11)

The implications are clear. Although each school has a responsibility to raise standards under government policy (challenge children to do better), no school on its own can make effective provision for the complexity and range of children's needs on one hand and their 'extraordinary talents' on the other. Barber is saying that young people's education cannot be limited to the school they enter at the age of eleven, if all their aspirations are to be raised.

This is the purpose of the core 'networks' belief in Excellence in Cities and the expectation behind the organisation of aspects of its programme. Schools that have developed their strengths by becoming specialist or beacon schools or city learning centres are expected to offer programmes or courses to children attending other schools, perhaps through the area's programme for the gifted and talented. Similarly, schools that have particular strengths in coaching teachers or pupils on the matter of challenging behaviour can host a Learning Support Unit. Some schools may have more than one strength to offer the wider school community, just as they can have more than one specialism.

The level of collaboration required for this vision to become reality is of quite a different order from that required for the occasional joint professional development day in a school cluster, or for the programme provided by an individual specialist secondary school to a number of partner primary and special schools. A wide range of provision for children has to be planned, and this was required from the beginning of local education authorities and their schools receiving Excellence in Cities funding. A *partnership board* had to be established that included representatives of all the secondary schools, the local education authority and other significant partners such as further education colleges. The Excellence in Cities plan for the area that required DfES approval was the plan submitted by this partnership, not the local authority. The partnership board had to decide which schools would be given each of the large resources associated with the programme – for example specialist status, or the City Learning Centres – and, importantly, how the partnership would be served by them. Such decisions sometimes went to a vote and the heads of potential specialist schools or City Learning Centres needed to consult the heads of other schools in the city or borough. Time will tell whether Excellence in Cities has indeed led to effective cross-city or cross-borough programmes, available to children 'whether they have special needs or have extraordinary talent', but the policy intention represents a clear break with the previous government's.

When set against the context of the quasi-market with its autonomous, frequently isolated schools, it is clear that the significance of this policy development was both understood and deliberate:

> In the *Excellence in Cities* areas we are also seeking a new approach to decision-making, with the secondary schools in an area working collaboratively with the Education Authority and thinking strategically – collaborating, rather than competing. (Blunkett, 2000a, p11/12)

And as we have seen, collaboration is also the expectation in a number of other important areas of government policy – specialist schools, the pathfinders for diversity, and the 14-19 initiative (the latter depending on it for success). It was required of the schools in the original free-standing Education Action Zones, even though the joint Action Forum in only one of them took on the voluntarily ceded powers of schools' governing bodies. It is an expectation of the Leadership Incentive Grant, where *Leadership Collaboratives* are required (DfES, 2002d). And it is the object of study in the National College for School Leadership's project on networked learning communities (DfES, 2003a).

Collaboration is easiest to achieve physically in large urban areas, where far more secondary schools are within reasonable travelling distance. It will be much more difficult elsewhere, although this is what the national policy intends. In non-urban areas, however, comprehensive schools are in less danger of acquiring bottom strata characteristics because there are fewer of them and they generally have a broad social intake (Brighouse, 2002).

The vision of urban collaboration inherent in Excellence in Cities, in which schools together provide for the diverse range of 'special needs or extraordinary talents', enrolling outsiders such as high achievers, business mentors or prestigious universities, is potentially exciting. The comprehensive principle is being re-defined. It can no longer be realised by individual schools, only by groups of schools or the whole service of a city or borough.

Against the persistent background of the crisis narrative, this is an inspiring message. In the final chapter I discuss whether these significant initiatives will successfully counteract learning disadvantage in the context of the quasi-market.

There are some less positive things to be said about *Excellence in Cities*. As a programme, it offers little guidance on pedagogy. The key stage 3 strategy was meant to fill this gap. The six strands, promoted to deal with a number of important matters in bottom strata schools such as behaviour and disaffection, are all compulsory; all schools in the designated areas have to implement them in the ways prescribed. Even when strands are welcomed by the schools – which they usually are – they are not formulated on the basis of the collective needs analysis recommended in chapters 6 and 7, based on the study of the children and the communities the schools serve. This has implications for the level of change achieved in the classrooms of *Excellence in Cities* schools and the development of sufficient reflective school capacity, which is more difficult anyway in bottom strata schools because of their context for learning and teaching (see chapter 7). So it remains to be seen whether *Excellence in Cities* will be a positive contribution to change or a hindrance, just another of the multiple initiatives schools have to manage. The Tribal Education (2002) study was commissioned to provide advice in just such a context.

Continuity and change

To complete the picture, we need to look at the three documents published while this book was being written: *Time for Standards* (DfES, 2002c) issued in autumn 2002, *A New Specialist System: Transforming Secondary Education* (DfES, 2003a) issued in February 2003 and *Excellence and Enjoyment – A Strategy for Primary Schools* (DfES, 2003b) issued in May.

Time for Standards is the latest document in the 'workforce remodelling' discussions that have gone on ever since the *Teachers Green Paper* (DfEE, 1998d) ushered in performance management. It was accompanied by documents on teacher workload and the balance of responsibilities between teaching and support staff that were intended to lead to reductions nationally in teachers' workload and create the time for standards signalled in the title. An agreement was signed with all but one of the teacher trade unions in early 2003 which would lead among other things to guaranteed non-contact time for teachers. If this is eventually achieved, it will undoubtedly help create some extra capacity for reflection on practice. It will also change conceptions of the work in many primary classrooms, as for at least 10 per cent of each week the children will be taught by someone other than their regular class teacher. The use of setting has already produced some changes of this sort (Ofsted, 1999a).

The comments of the workforce remodelling document on the direction of government reform, following the evaluation of the national literacy and numeracy strategies (Earl *et al*, 2003) are significant. The implications of the document are potentially encouraging for bottom strata schools to develop as reflective, learning schools, able to counter learning disadvantage. The document signalled the need for change away from what it calls the 'informed prescription' (p11) of 1997 to 'informed professionalism' (p10). High levels of prescription, according to *Time for Standards*, can create 'bureaucracy, stress and increased workloads' (p11). It calls instead for:

> more fundamental reform which puts teachers and heads centre stage. They are best placed to understand the needs of individual pupils and the often complex interplay of factors which affect learning at a local level... We need to empower teachers and heads, allowing them to use their skills to create increasingly differentiated and individualised learning pathways and to stimulate school-led innovation...To develop a pedagogy fit for the twenty-first century, we need to restore more autonomy and professional control to teachers, albeit within a national system of accountability. (*ibid*)

With respect to the development of 'new models of teaching and learning', the document recommends:

> Greater use of pedagogic strategies which develop students' learning capabilities ... use of student feedback ... a commitment to sharing best practice ... more effective team working (and) increasingly innovative and flexible timetables and class structures. (p12)

It stresses the need to ensure that 'our approach to pedagogy is consistent' and asks (p13) how 'we can develop a consistent pedagogy'.

Greater autonomy, this book has argued, is necessary for the development of learning schools so this shift away from prescription appears promising. So long as the 'consistent pedagogy' is not a uniform national pedagogy, this policy shift could also take account of what is known about learning and its local complexities (chapter

5). *Time for Standards* appears to signal a new approach. But it offers no policies to help build the capacity in schools for teacher reflection that is essential for practice and for Fullan's third level of change (2001a). Neither does it suggest that the pressure on bottom strata schools will be reduced, beyond the extra time to be provided through the remodelling reforms. It does mention national training programmes for the key stage 3 strategy and the use of ICT, but these build capacity of a different kind than the reflective sort. The prospect of better teamwork is offered, but it will depend upon teachers and support staff working together better as a result of the reforms.

A New Specialist System (DfES, 2003a) expressed general sentiments much like those of *Time for Standards*. Under the heading 'A New Phase of Reform' (p10), it states that 'we recognise ...we need to build a new relationship with schools, headteachers and governors'. Schools need 'more freedom and flexibility in the way they use their resources, in the way they design the curriculum and in the teaching methods they use' within a framework of accountability. Reform is 'a shared endeavour', and

> ... we can see from many examples across the country that when schools are given encouragement and support, they can and do achieve great things for their schools and communities. (p11)

A large section entitled 'Partnerships beyond the classroom' (p35) explains that raising attainment is a shared responsibility and that effective partnerships with parents are required, echoing Earl *et al*. Extending the school day is mooted and further funding was promised for out-of-school-hours learning. Both are consistent with the learning and teaching approaches discussed in chapter 5 and 6.

Excellence and Enjoyment (DfES, 2003b) was intended by its title to signal the nature of the new primary strategy. It absorbs rather than replaces the national literacy and numeracy strategies, extending its interest to teaching in all subjects. It takes heed of Earl *et al* (2003), but scarcely mentions the national evaluation, Ofsted's comments about creativity in good schools (2002b) or the concerns expressed about targets and pressures. The document makes a strong quasi-market defence of performance tables (p20) and of targets, shifting the 2004 targets to 2006 and making them more of an aspiration.

Excellence and Enjoyment says that target-setting would begin with schools in future, not local education authorities, potentially reducing the high stakes pressure Earl *et al* identified. The test results for seven year olds are to be downgraded. Generally, there was an emphasis on increasing school autonomy, easing the burden of planning and fostering greater creativity by teachers and schools.

What is significant for bottom strata schools?

And so to conclusions. The national framework within which schools work, especially when legislation is as detailed as it is in England, offers little stability. Many of the policy initiatives described in this chapter will take at least five years to be fully implemented. By then, things will have changed again and matters will be seen in a different light.

Meanwhile learning disadvantage remains a huge barrier to raising achievement and increases in severity as pupils move through the system. In the last chapter of this book, I assess what is significant in the developing national framework and the potential contribution of national policies to supporting the work of bottom strata schools. Will they be able to develop as learning schools and come to understand and address learning disadvantage in their communities? Will they be freed from the crisis narrative? The conclusions I draw are of the moment, but although they might need revising in the light of further developments, my concern is to identify the right trends so that they can be established at the start.

Chapter 9
Schools for our cities:
current trends, future prospects

Learning disadvantage and social justice

This book has argued that a profound process of school stratification has occurred in the UK over the past thirty years, caused by social and economic decline in urban areas and the flight by middle class and other parents from the schools built to serve them. The consequence is that many of the schools in our major cities, particularly at secondary level, are attended by a disproportionate number of pupils unlikely to attain national benchmarks by the time they leave. Because of their origin in the stratification process, I call these schools bottom strata schools.

The social and material disadvantage endemic around bottom strata schools results in learning disadvantage for many of their pupils, often the majority. Disadvantage arises from the nature of learning and the interplay between its processes in school and out. Even if they are not subject to social and material disadvantage, pupils who cannot draw fully on their informal learning in their family and community to support their school work will suffer learning disadvantage. This is as relevant for schools in mono-ethnic working class communities as for those in culturally diverse communities, with their varied cultural traditions and assumptions. Bottom strata schools are all different and the task of each is unique.

Because the context for learning and teaching is difficult, it is harder to raise aspirations or improve educational outcomes than in schools that have more balanced social intakes or serve more advantaged areas. Yet it is in bottom strata schools most of all that improvement is needed if children are to enter adult life on an equal footing with their contemporaries elsewhere. The older pupils are before their learning disadvantage begins to be tackled, the harder it is to intervene effectively and the greater the gap will be between their attainment and that of their peers in more fortunate circumstances. Unsuccessful learning is cyclical. And it is reinforced by poor experiences outside school. The life experiences and decisions of the families of these young people can too easily continue to the next generation, so perpetuating poverty.

Countering learning disadvantage is one of the most potent contributions schools make to social justice. The conventions and ways of learning in the community must be the starting points for the learning experiences planned for children from the moment they begin school. Parents and the community need to be enrolled in the school's mission so they make active contributions to fulfilling it. All young people need to be able to develop as self-confident and skilled learners.

This means that schools have to learn from the community and children about the community they serve, and it means each school needs to become a learning school, rooted in reflection as the basis for improvement. The process of becoming a learning school is one of ever-more skilled exploration and of learning. Entering the sorts of partnership described in chapters 6 and 7 to do so requires patience, realism and capacity.

Schools can make a major contribution to countering learning disadvantage, but they cannot do it on their own. They need close working relationships with the other agencies working in the community. Building them requires time and patience, as they too have to be based on learning.

I am not arguing for dismantling national frameworks for accountability. However, schools need enough autonomy to be able to develop in their own ways, reflecting and responding to the requirements of the communities they serve. How bottom strata schools are regulated and judged should be designed to help rather than hinder them in this task. Sadly, the demanding work the schools must do is often impeded by public discourse that feeds on the crisis narrative, used by politicians, the media or parents.

This concluding chapter identifies the trends in the UK which may help bottom strata schools eradicate learning disadvantage and those which might hinder them. It looks at the developments that are still needed and evaluates the chances they will be achieved. And it considers whether we have seen the end of the crisis narrative.

Current reforms: helps and hindrances

The UK government is currently providing much assistance to schools in their efforts to counter learning disadvantage. Thinking skills, for instance, are intended to be an integral part of the national curriculum (DfEE and QCA, 1999). Numerous publications and training courses offer guidance to teachers and schools on learning techniques and how the brain works. Many initiatives are funded through the national programmes discussed in chapter 8.

Partnerships are increasingly being formed between universities, local education authorities and schools, providing support for accredited study and research into learning and the community. Myriad projects are funded through national and local programmes to help schools address aspects of learning disadvantage (under a variety of labels). And many more opportunities for out-of-school learning are funded by these schemes and the New Opportunities Fund. Such investment has fostered a growth in after-school clubs and other study support provision in which young people (and teachers) can experience different approaches to learning, so supporting effective learning transfer. The enhanced funding available to schools through all the recent schemes and programmes has created new supportive initiatives in urban areas.

Schools themselves have received increases in revenue funding through their local education authority and directly from central government. School capital expenditure has also increased dramatically since 1998.

But although many developments are bound to help the educational aims argued for in this book, there are also many hindrances, some of them severe. Teachers and schools need time to develop their learning but this is in short supply. Teachers in England work an average 52 hour week, of which roughly a third (35 per cent) is spent teaching (DfES, 2002c). The rest is spent on preparation, non-teaching contact, administration and management. It remains to be seen whether the national workforce agreement will reduce the pressure on teachers and whether they will take advantage of any extra time to develop their work.

Pressures created by accountability requirements can discourage innovation in any but the bravest schools. These pressures discourage exploration of the roots of the learning disadvantage at the heart of many attainment problems. Will the new Ofsted inspection framework give credit to individual schools' explorations or adequately recognise the messy process of change and the likelihood of frequent setbacks? Will there be a new national climate of mature, open debate about urban education or will the national discourse still be about crisis?

Even the increases in funding aroused controversy. Rises in revenue funding have often been accompanied by increasing costs and new responsibilities, such as implementing workforce remodelling. Capital funding, while never higher, has provoked controversy because the government prefers the private sector to be involved in major projects (Audit Commission, 2003).

Primary reform

In primary schools, many teachers need to re-learn ways of thinking professionally, reflect on their practice and become used to doing so as a matter of course. Although many teachers already modify the requirements of the national literacy and numeracy strategies for the specific needs of their children (Earl *et al,* 2003), others cannot because their learning has not reached an appropriate stage. Persistent national pressure on schools for reform will impede further teacher learning, making it more difficult for schools to attend to their learning capacity, essential for tackling learning disadvantage.

Although there are signs that the government sees the need for some change in direction, emphasising a new relationship with heads and teachers and an encouragement of creativity (DfES, 2002c, 2003a and 2003b), the performance tables and targets remain in place, although targets are now determined by the schools.

Secondary reform

Secondary reform has had less classroom prescription and a longer time scale for implementation. It includes positive opportunities for bottom strata schools. Moreover, elements of the reform such as the development of bids for specialist status can be used as vehicles to counter learning disadvantage because they have to be preceded by a period of reflection by the school on their current and potential strengths.

However, the problems concerning capacity and time for learning are compounded by the concentrated pressure on bottom strata schools arising from the very nature of the reform and its national implementation. Leaving aside its prescriptive nature, *Excellence in Cities* is an extensive programme with large planning and resource implications. Each aspect of the programme needs a plan, often a coordinator and always management capacity, which may be in short supply. When the additional requirements that arise from being identified as a school 'Facing Challenging Circumstances' are taken into account and added to those for the *Leadership Incentive Grant* (DfES, 2002d), the demands become remorseless. And if a school is also experiencing difficulty or 'causing concern', yet more planning and resource requirements might be imposed on it by the local education authority or following an Ofsted inspection.

Such detailed requirements are all part of the intended 'high challenge' of the reform to raise standards, just as the considerably enhanced resources available to urban schools are part of the 'high support'. But even when the government is striving to achieve coherence nationally, schools typically have to produce a series of plans, sometimes with different timescales, different formats and different targets which may then have to be integrated. All these plans require detailed tracking, so significant developments might well be lost in the detail. The pressure for reform and educational improvement, though admirable, can manifest itself as pressure for bureaucratic compliance. And it is hard for schools with the least capacity to integrate all these different aspirations successfully, however much they agree with them, into a coherent overall school vision developed with the community that reflects the specific circumstances of the school.

The danger is that externally required developments might not be properly thought through by the school. Instead, bureaucratic compliance might be achieved by concentrating on short term goals, sometimes imposed from outside, making the transition to school-determined goals more problematic. For example, the imperative of raising attainment on key benchmarks as quickly as possible – sometimes to escape the 'Challenging Circumstances' label with its potential threat of closure – may lead to resources being concentrated on the year 11 students who are performing on the C/D GCSE grade borderline. Such a concentration may be appropriate, but it will not improve learning outcomes in the long term; coherence can only come from embedding such measures in the school's self-determined long term vision.

Six developments that will be required

Only careful monitoring will tell whether the positive statements of *A New Specialist System* and *Excellence and Enjoyment* will generate a more constructive pace and pressure for change on bottom strata schools and enable them to develop capacity and adequate time for their own learning more easily. Will life feel different for staff in primary and secondary schools, because of the shift in emphasis indicated in these recent publications?

Other developments are also essential. This book has grappled with the complexities of bottom strata schools and shown clearly that it will take more than one approach or strategy to enable them to be as effective as possible. I conclude with consideration of six major developments which, taken together, might succeed in tackling their specific needs and raising educational standards for all.

The first two concern the schools themselves and argue for the desirability of self-determined rather than outside pressure and the allocation of dedicated time for working towards change. The third is concerned with tackling the quasi-market and the resulting stratification and argues that, while fundamental change is unlikely, programmes like Excellence in Cities can be used to create a more level playing field over time so must continue.

The last three developments are concerned with thought, perception and image. I discuss possibilities for a new and radical vision for secondary education, ending or at least moderating the use of the crisis narrative and, finally, the need for teachers to construct new mental models of the 'good' school before they can make their own school a good one.

1. Creating pressure of a different kind

The greater emphasis on school autonomy is to be welcomed but pressure is still needed in the system to prevent the routinisation described in chapter 6. This pressure on schools to improve has however to be more sophisticated than the current formula of Ofsted inspection, high stakes testing and performance tables and government prescription.

What is needed is pressure driven by positive professional expectation generated by the schools themselves, as they develop their ambitions in collaboration with their communities and with each other. Improvement must start with individual and institutional learning. Bottom strata schools should be invited to take the lead in setting the pace for change, thus securing the acknowledgment of their importance to raising the achievement of all children nationally.

It is appropriate for school staff and communities to generate repertoires for exploring and countering learning disadvantage within national frameworks. Voluntary local, regional or national networks of schools should be facilitated and resourced, thus creating wider professional learning communities with a common focus on disadvantage. These networks would be recruited from among enthusiasts – always the best agents of effective change – and from schools which are already successful or ambitious to become so.

Not all schools will be ready to respond to such an invitation and the new networks should be created with care. They need to be voluntary associations with a common focus, unlike *Excellence in Cities* (DfEE, 1999a) or Education Action Zones which are also driven by accountability and external pressure because of their compulsory inclusivity.

The major cities in the UK with their large numbers of bottom strata schools have a vested interest in making high quality state education accessible to all. Even one high status national network of learning developing bottom strata schools could powerfully redefine our national aspirational picture of good schooling in much the same way that the new chartered status in the London Challenge will begin to change perceptions of teaching. Both may mark a radical departure from the idea of suburban schools with foundation status serving socially advantaged areas as the ideal school model in the quasi-market.

2. Finding the time for curriculum change

If bottom strata schools are to be the leaders of change, they need to be able to find the curriculum time to address learning disadvantage (see chapter 6). Their pupils are unlikely to be the children who will be quickest to develop as self-confident and skilled learners: they need time to catch up and, where possible, be given experiences comparable to those middle class children enjoy.

The two year 6 boys from Bristol illustrate the contrast. The boy who has graduate parents and the prospect of a private secondary education brings to his schooling self-confidence, transferable learning and an expectation of success. It derives from his experience out of school, the time he spends talking about it with his family and friends and the greater facility thus generated for using language to support learning. The other boy is distracted by aspects of his family circumstances and needs the time and opportunity to develop the self-efficacy in his learning that he can transfer to his out-of-school context and later life. Only his experiences in the school curriculum could enable this to happen and this process needs to begin as early as possible in his schooling. It may be difficult to close the gap in their learning advantage completely – though this is worth striving for – but the gap can be narrowed.

Parts of the curriculum in bottom strata schools will have to be reduced to allow this work to take place. The question is: what should go? Traditionally in schools serving disadvantaged areas, the broad curriculum has been sacrificed to a narrow focus on basic skills (Hallinger and Murphy, 1986; Haberman, 1991; Teddlie and Stringfield, 1993; Thrupp, 1999). The original literacy and numeracy pilots in urban areas in the mid-1990s were partly driven by such ideas.

But the solution is more complicated than a straight substitution. Although the need for children to practise particular aspects of learning may require extra curriculum time, it cannot be just an add-on that demands of teachers still longer hours. What is required is greater flexibility in the implementation of the national curriculum and further reductions in the subject requirements, which are already somewhat eased by recent reforms.

We know that imaginative primary schools already modify how they provide the national curriculum to stimulate their pupils (Ofsted, 2000b) and that effective schools still maintain a broad curriculum (Ofsted, 2002b). This suggests that more flexibility exists than most schools avail themselves of. But it is insufficient or not well enough understood to enable bottom strata schools to take full advantage.

So some of the curriculum flexibility being allowed post-14 would be welcome for earlier age provision. As this seems unlikely at present, schools must at least be encouraged to create greater flexibility for themselves within existing frameworks. Do they need to cover so much detail in order to receive a good Ofsted report? Is the current level of detailed planning in schools – a legacy from the late 1980s of prescription and high stakes accountability – essential? Schools need to take greater risks and local education authorities and central government should be encouraging them to do so. As with all effective national change, development needs to take place at all levels and not just be driven from the top (Fullan, 2001a). Out of school experiences need to be provided in greater quantities in bottom strata schools so they can be used to close the gap in transferability of learning.

3. Changing stratification and the quasi-market

Learning disadvantage is concentrated in certain schools because of the stratification produced by the quasi-market. So what can be done about it? Drastic change seems unlikely. Radically dismantling the quasi-market would be extremely risky for any government, particularly as school transfer in cities causes parents so much anxiety. The expectation of 'choice' and the narratives of reproduction are deeply ingrained, particularly among middle class parents. All that can be realistically hoped for is some modification. National policy should address the way urban schools are perceived among parents, modify the most harmful aspects of school market behaviour, and reduce the effects on children of stratification by reducing their learning disadvantage.

Some trends in government policy since 1997 have tried to address both parental perceptions and the effects of school stratification in urban areas; policy does appear to reflect a recognition of what has happened in our cities. The principle of retaining 'aspirant parents' in the state sector through Excellence in Cities, and particularly the gifted and talented strand, is aimed at reducing stratification. But measures such as establishing more Learning Support Units, restricting re-admission to school of certain children after they have been permanently excluded (Clarke, 2002) and the standards agenda as a whole should also be seen in this light. All these strands are concerned with making state schools more acceptable to greater numbers of middle class parents in urban areas, in the hope that schools will be changed by having a broader intake. If the measures are successful, the attendance of more of these children will broaden the social mix in urban schools and in time the harmful effects of stratification will diminish.

The requirements for collaboration should build a scenario that is quite different from the professional isolation of schools that is endemic in the extreme manifestations of the quasi-market, sometimes deliberately sought through grant maintained status. The requirement (and experience) of planning together may well modify some of the school market behaviour Ball graphically described (1994), although the evidence is yet to be collected. This change may also contribute to the 'district-wide' basis for change that Fullan (2001a) considered so vital.

The most important current question is whether the provision being developed through Excellence in Cities will alleviate the effects of stratification on children now, as opposed to when there might be a greater social mix in schools. In terms of making specific additional provision for some of them in their schools, learning disadvantage will in one sense be reduced, but whether the wider concept of needs and talents outlined by Barber (2000a) will be realised needs to be looked at as part of the wider vision for urban education.

Excellence in Cities will make a difference because the experience of joint provision will affect many more children permanently than previous joint provision such as city-wide dance festivals. There is the potential for some alleviation of the effects of narrow social mix with more children being afforded more frequent access to learning in different contexts. Specifically, there will be more opportunities for children from bottom strata schools to meet children from other schools who are socially and educationally accustomed to expecting and experiencing success. This is important for the success of young people in bottom strata schools (Thrupp, 1999). Being successful alongside 'aspirant' children might afford them glimpses of their own potential, in turn affecting what they bring back to their class-mates.

So all these measures are worth pursuing as they may well modify the effects of stratification in cities. However, a fundamental change in the context described in chapter 4 and to stratification as des-cribed in chapter 3 will, if it does happen, take time.

4. Developing a different vision for secondary education

The shift in national policy towards wanting urban school systems as a whole to make appropriate provision for all children because no school can do it alone should drive new policy. This means a new and workable definition of comprehensive schooling for the twenty-first century that commands wide assent and creates a greater sense of collective purpose.

A collective purpose approach to comprehensive education has been expressed in connection with Excellence in Cities initiatives but it does not appear in *A New Specialist System* (DfES, 2003a). There is no good reason why such a vision could not be articulated, even though any government has to acknowledge the aspirations of a wide range of stakeholders in their pronouncements. But to articulate it would require full public discussion of the nature of stratification in cities. It is high time such discussion took place, even though there will be difficulties with stakeholders who oppose comprehensives and possibly also with staff and parents whose children are in super-selective and selective schools (Newsam, 1998).

Problems cannot be addressed until they are publicly acknowledged. The goals of urban school systems need to be clearly articulated rather than left to chance or unexpectedly revealed at certain meetings. Visions and missions cannot be only tacitly understood. Changes could easily be made nationally without undermining local work on collective visions for countering learning disadvantage if the government believed in such an approach. The staff, governors and students in bottom strata schools would feel better about their own work of dismantling learning disadvantage if this change were supported by government. Instead of being seen as holding back the national mission, their major contribution to it would be clearly perceived.

A radical vision – collegiates
An even more democratic and radical vision of collaboration has been put forward by Tim Brighouse, the London Schools Commissioner (Brighouse, 2002). The fully developed collegiate academies he advocates would include private schools and possibly schools outside the UK. He envisages one collegiate admission process and one collegiate set of examination results for the performance tables. The concept of the 'home' school would change. And, in its wake, so would the nature of stratification and the quasi-market.

This is hugely ambitious and has immense policy implications, but the intention is that collegiates begin as local voluntary arrangements, such as the Birmingham 14-19 pathfinder, and the notion put forward here of national networks of bottom strata schools. When groups of schools experience success in particular endeavours, they can progress to the next steps and avail themselves of further opportunities. Parents in some urban areas could hardly be more anxious about secondary school choice than they are now and this may well make them receptive to ambitious new ideas.

Obstacles to the achievement of a new vision
The reality is that there are obstacles to the achievement of new visions, whether of the kinds of collaboration suggested in this book or collegiates. The change in focus that would be demanded of secondary headteachers and their senior staff accustomed to operating in the untrammelled quasi-market is immense. And collabora-

tion between schools is hard work, resource-intensive and may well involve conflict. Bottom strata schools all have vulnerable times when it is just not possible for senior staff to leave the premises during school hours, and this makes full or consistent participation difficult. Primary schools would find it particularly difficult.

However, effective networks can provide understanding and support for schools that find it difficult to participate. All schools have rough patches and it is understood that 'problems do not stay solved... you have to learn to do the right thing over and over again' (Fullan, 2001a, p270). Change is constant but uneven; setbacks are common. Time and patience are essential.

Only a minority of children will benefit directly from even the most developed collaborative programmes, although a greater number may be indirectly affected. For those involved, schooling will improve, and the benefits may trickle down to others. But a firm foundation for the systematic exploration of learning disadvantage needs to be established at each school. Although this is vital it will not be easy to do.

Stakeholders throughout the system will have their reservations. Not all parents will be convinced about the value of wider school networks or even the concept of specialisation. Those at the top of the pecking order will probably continue to want their children to be learning with 'people like us' and middle class parents may find it difficult to accept an admissions process for collegiates in which they have less say. The changed nature of a local school will concern parents and staff and the prospect of phalanxes of students aged 14-19 travelling round cities will not immediately appeal. So all these developments, like all change, may create potential dissatisfaction and conflict. If some can be persuaded to take the risk, however, successful outcomes will persuade others. This will take time, but we should start now.

Whatever happens, there will always be schools in the bottom strata, even when some of the effects of the quasi-market and stratification are ultimately ameliorated and more children of aspirant parents attend urban state schools. The schools' harsh context for learning may improve and they may develop approaches to countering learning disadvantage, but their essence will remain the same unless wider social and economic changes are made. The origins of strati-fication lie outside schools. Current government policy seeks to alleviate or eliminate child poverty by 2019, but the contexts for learning and teaching will persist in some measure for another generation.

Limitations of the Academies and new private schools

Through their greater freedoms, Academies may be able to explore new approaches to pedagogy, curriculum, accreditation pathways and the shape of the school day and year, just as City Technology Colleges did, but without their potential exclusivity. The new organisation and possibilities in an individual school could provide a psychological fillip to staff and attract children from a wider variety of social backgrounds. But though this will benefit indivi-dual schools, the broader contribution to change requires collabora-tion and the creation of a wider-district focus.

Even where Academies are willing to collaborate, they will find it dif-ficult because of their radically different accountability mechanisms. They are not part of a local target-setting process, for example, how-ever low key this may now become, and they would not be a full member of the Excellence in Cities partnership. With their board of trustees and direct accountability to the DfES, similar to that of the former grant maintained schools, leadership teams in academies will not have time to participate fully in two different frameworks. This has implications for the *London Challenge* (Morris, 2002b) and its pro-posed thirty new Academies.

What might be called the new private schools will encounter similar obstacles. The 2002 Education Act made local education authorities responsible for inviting a variety of promoters to express an interest when a new school is being considered, for demographic or strategic reasons, 'particularly .... in areas where there is underachievement' (DfES, 2003a, p21). These promoters could include 'parent and community groups, private and charitable companies, voluntary groups including church and faith communities, those offering dis-tinctive educational philosophies, and existing schools or consortia of schools' (*ibid*). Some LEAs have already sought such arrange-ments for schools in difficulty. Whether these schools can deliver the collaboration the government hopes for in its diversity programme (see chapter 8) will depend on their arrangements for governance and their context.

5. Ending the crisis narrative

The crisis narrative, with its message that schools in the cities are poor because the staff are poor, has already done too much damage. National politicians and their officials need to take a lead in challenging the crisis narrative. It will never disappear completely, because of the picture presented by the mass media and the perceptions of parents about their choice of school. But the story must be less destructive.

There is evidence that the use of the crisis narrative is already reducing and becoming less harsh. Early in 2003, for example, a government minister talked about public service defining the soul of the nation (Miliband, 2003). He praised teachers who had received honours in the New Year's list and said that the 'ethic of public service symbolised by these people is precious' (p1). The celebration of successful teaching practice and respect for teachers was talked about even while the next stages of reform were being outlined. The three government publications discussed at the end of chapter 8 (DfES, 2002c, 2003a and 2003b) all had a positive tone, even as they announced further change and stressed the need to tackle poor performance.

Only time will tell whether positive comments and change of tone will have any effect and whether schools will be accorded greater professional autonomy. More fundamentally, will staff in schools feel less pressured and less subject to attrition? Will they feel more empowered to be creative and take the initiative? Can they be won over to a national mission? It is not possible to say as yet, but the public reaction to a letter a minister recently wrote to primary schools (Twigg, 2003) is telling.

This famous letter precipitated a flurry of concerned replies to newspapers and the educational press. The Minister began by praising the 'impressive achievements of primary schools in raising standards since the introduction of the national literacy and numeracy strategies', before pointing out the 'wide variation in results of schools in similar circumstances' and claiming that 'we currently have concerns about the rates of progress that pupils are making between key stage 1 and 2 in about one in four schools'. He said that the 'Government was determined to see significant improvements in 2003 and beyond' and was 'committed to supporting schools in achieving the highest possible standards', and listed the support available.

Although much of the letter was factual, it was received as more finger-wagging about 'improving leadership'. Even though teachers generally welcome the changes in the national literacy and numeracy strategies (Earl *et al,* 2003), for example, this cameo of public reaction indicates how far we still are from full, emotional enrolment in a national mission. There appears to be some change, but people are still sceptical.

6. Schools for our cities: developing new mental models

As we pursue new national visions, explore the nature of learning disadvantage and advance our own learning, we need to reappraise the mental models we hold of a good school. The notion of the good school suffuses the quasi-market and insinuates itself into the staffrooms of bottom strata schools. Staff may believe the best schools to be traditionalist foundation or independent and consequently see themselves providing an inferior education for their pupils. Worse, they may believe that they are doing the best they can in the circumstances.

Such mental models are stubborn. If staff are reflective and understand that the task of each school is unique, they will understand that good schools and classrooms have to look different. But overturning entrenched beliefs is difficult and often lonely. Yet only by throwing out such traditional mental models will staff bring self-belief to their classrooms.

Government has a vital role. It frames the national discourse about education and it promotes images of successful classrooms and schools and decides how they are measured. These images need to be more varied than they are now. But we all bear some responsibility and must be prepared to challenge our own beliefs about good schooling and promote publicly the excellence we find in bottom strata schools. What is more, we need to stand by what we say.

The development of the young people at the centre of this book into self-confident learners will be most effective when all those who work in or with bottom strata schools believe in the worth of the task. This is not charity. The task is to achieve social justice and a school system in which all children, irrespective of their social or material circumstances, are able to learn to the full.

Bibliography

Anyon, J and Wilson, W (1997) *Ghetto Schooling – A Political Economy of Urban Educational Reform* New York: Teachers' College Press

Arnot, M, Gray, J, James, M and Rudduck, J with Duveen, G (1998) *Recent Research on Gender and Educational Performance* London: HMSO with the permission of Ofsted

ATD Fourth World (2000) *Education: Opportunities Lost: The Education System as experienced by Families Living in Poverty* London: ATD Fourth World

Atkinson, T and Claxton, G (2000) Introduction to Atkinson, T and Claxton, G (Eds) *The Intuitive Practitioner – On the Value of Not Always Knowing What One is Doing* Buckingham: Open University Press

Audit Commission (2003) *PFI in Schools – The Quality and Cost of Buildings and Services provided by early Private Finance Initiative Schemes* London: The Audit Commission

Ayers, W (2001) *To Teach – The Journey of a Teacher* New York: Teachers College Press, Columbia University

Ayers, W and Ford, P (Eds) (1996) *City Kids City Teachers – Reports from the Front Row* New York: The New Press

Bagley, C, Woods, P and Glatter, R (2001) Rejecting Schools: Towards a Fuller Understanding of the Process of Parental Choice *School Leadership and Management* 21 (3) pages 309-325

Ball, S (1994) *Education Reform – A Critical and Post-structural Approach* Buckingham: Open University Press

Ball, S (2003) *Class Strategies and the Education Market – The Middle Classes and Social Advantage* London: RoutledgeFalmer

Ball, S, Bowe R and Gewirtz, S (1995) Circuits of Schooling: A Sociological Exploration of Parental Choice of School in Social-Class *Contexts The Sociological Review* 43 p52-18 reproduced in Halsey *et al* (1997)

Barber, M (1996a) *The Learning Game: Arguments for an Educational Revolution* London: Victor Gollancz

Barber, M (1996b) *Creating a Framework for Success in Urban Areas* In Barber, M and Dann, R (Eds)

Barber, M (1997) *How to do the Impossible – a Guide for Politicians with a Passion for Education* London: Institute of Education

Barber, M (1998) *The Dark Side of the Moon: Imagining an end to Failure in Urban*

Education In Stoll and Myers

Barber, M (2000a) The Very Big Picture *Improving Schools* 3 (2), pages 5-17

Barber, M (2000b) Large-Scale Reform is Possible *Education Week* 20 (11), page 39

Barber, M and Dann, R (Eds) (1996) *Raising Educational Standards in the Inner Cities* London: Cassell

Bernstein, B (1975) *Class, Codes and Control Volume 3 – Towards a Theory of Educational Transmissions* London: Routledge and Kegan Paul

Black, P and Wiliam, D (1998) *Inside the Black Box – Raising Standards through Classroom Assessment* London: King's College School of Education

Blair, T (2002) At Our Best when at our Boldest – Speech to the Labour Party Conference, 1st October From the Labour Party website – www.labour.org.uk

Blatchford, P (1996) Pupils' Views on School Work and School from 7 to 16 Years *Research Papers in Education* 11 (3) p263-288

Blunkett, D (2000a) Raising Aspirations in the 21st Century – a Speech Given to the North of England Conference London: DfEE

Blunkett, D (2000b) *Transforming Secondary Education* London: the Social Market Foundation

Bradshaw, J (Ed) (2002) *The Well-being of Children in the UK* Plymouth: Save the Children

Brighouse, T (2002) Comprehensive Schools Then, Now and in the Future – Is it Time to Draw a Line in the Sand and Create a New Ideal? Text of the Caroline Benn, Brian Simon Memorial Lecture, given at the Institute of Education, 28 September

Bristol Local Education Authority (2000) The Policy and Directions for Secondary Education in Bristol – A General Discussion Paper. A Consultation paper produced for the Cabinet October, 2000

Bristol Local Education Authority (2001) Transforming Secondary Education in Bristol – Proposals and Recommendations prepared by the Director of Education and Lifelong Learning Report to Bristol City Council November, 2001

Broadfoot, P, Osborn, M, Planel, C and Sharpe, K (2000) *Promoting Quality in Learning – does England have the Answer? Findings from the Quest Project* London: Cassell

Brooker, L (2002) *Starting School – Young Children Learning Cultures* Buckingham: Open University Press

Brown, M (1998) *The Tyranny of the International Horse Race* in Slee *et al, op cit*

Brown, P and Lauder, H (1997) Education, Globalisation and Economic Development in Halsey *et al op cit*

Bruner, J (1996) *The Culture of Education* Cambridge, Mass: Harvard University Press

Buzan, T with Buzan, B (1993) *The Mindmap Book – Radiant Thinking, the Major Evolution in Human Thought* London: BBC

Campbell, C (Ed) (2002) *Developing Inclusive Schooling: Perspectives, Policies and Practices* London: Institute of Education, University of London

Campbell, C and Whitty, G (2002) *Inter-agency Collaborations for Inclusive Schooling* in Campbell *op cit* (Ed)

Church of England (2001) *The Way Ahead: Church of England Schools in the New Millennium* London: Church House Publishing

Clark, A (1993) *Homeless Children and their Access to Schooling – a Bristol Case Study* Bristol: The Space Trust

Clarke, C (2002) Discipline in Schools – Speech made to the Social Market Foundation London: DfES

Claxton, G (1997) *Hare Brain Tortoise Mind – Why Intelligence Increases When You Think Less* London: Fourth Estate Limited

Claxton, G (1999) *Wise Up – the Challenge of Lifelong Learning* London: Bloomsbury

Coldron, J and Williams, J (2000) Admission to Selective and Partially Selective Secondary Schools in England: A Critical Review of Practices. Paper presented to the British Education Research Association Conference Leeds, 2000

Coles, B and Kenwright, H (2002) *Educational Achievement* in Bradshaw, J. *op cit* (Ed)

Conservative Party (1997) *You Can Only be Sure with the Conservatives – Election Manifesto* London: The Conservative Party

Crook, D, Power, S and Whitty, G (1999) *The Grammar School Question – a Review of Research on Comprehensive and Selective Education* London: Institute of Education, University of London

De Bono, E (1986) *Six Thinking Hats* London: Viking

DfE (1992) *Choice and Diversity – a new Framework for Schools* London: HMSO

DfEE (1996) *Self-Government for Schools* London: HMSO

DfEE (1997a) *Excellence in Schools; a White Paper* London: The Stationery Office

DfEE (1997b) *The Implementation of the National Literacy Strategy* London: DfEE

DfEE (1998a) *New Procedures for Schools in Special Measures* London: DfEE

DfEE (1998b) *Code on LEA-School Relations* London: The Stationery Office

DfEE (1998c) *The Implementation of the National Numeracy Strategy* London: DfEE

DfEE (1998d) *Teachers – Meeting the Challenge of Change* London: The Stationery Office

DfEE (1998e) *The National Literacy Strategy – Framework for Teaching* London: DfEE

DfEE (1999a) *Excellence in Cities* London: The Stationery Office

DfEE (1999b) *The National Numeracy Strategy – Framework for Teaching Mathematics from Reception to Year 6* London: DfEE

DfEE and QCA (1999) *The National Curriculum: Handbook for Primary Teachers* (Also, *Handbook for Secondary Teachers*) London: DfEE and QCA

DfEE (2000) *Sure-Start* London: The Stationery Office

DfEE (2001) *Schools – Building on Success* London: The Stationery Office

DfES (2001) *Schools – Achieving Success* London: The Stationery Office

DfES (2002a) 14-19: *Extending Opportunities, Raising Standards* Consultation Document ('Green Paper') London: The Stationery Office

DfES (2002b) *Investing for Reform* Paper available on the DfES website from 16 July, following the announcement of the outcome of the comprehensive spending review London: DfES

DfES (2002c) *Time for Standards – Reforming the School Workforce* London: DfES

DfES (2002d) *Leadership Incentive Grant – Guidance* London: DfES

DfES (2003a) *A New Specialist System: Transforming Secondary Education* London: DfES

DfES (2003b) *Excellence and Enjoyment – a Strategy for Primary Schools* London: DfES

Dryden, G and Vos, J (1994) *The Learning Revolution – a Lifelong Learning Programme for the World's Finest Computer: Your Amazing Brain* Aylesbury: Accelerated Learning Systems Ltd

DWP (2002) *Opportunity for All: Fourth Annual Report 2002* London: The Stationery Office

Dyson, A and Robson, E (1999) *School, Family, Community – Mapping School Inclusion in the UK* Leicester: Youth Work Press/Joseph Rowntree Foundation

Earl, L, Watson, N, Levin, B, Leithwood, K, Fullan, M, and Torrance, N, with Jantzi, D, Mascall, B and Volante, L (2003) *Watching Learning 3 – Final Report of the External Evaluation of England's National Literacy and Numeracy Strategies* Torronto: Ontario Institute for Studies in Education, University of Toronto

Edmonds, R (1979) Effective Schools for the Urban Poor *Educational Leadership* 37 (1) p15-27

Edwards, T and Whitty, G (1997) Specialisation and Selection in Secondary Education *Oxford Review of Education* 23 (1) p5-15

Phillips, R and Furlong, J (Eds) (2002) *Education, Reform and the State: Twenty-five Years of Politics, Policy and Practice* London: Routledge/Falmer

Fimister, G (Ed) (2001) *Tackling Poverty in the UK – an End in Sight?* London: Child Poverty Action Group

Fullan, M (1993) *Change Forces – Probing the Depths of Educational Reform* London: Falmer Press

Fullan, M (2001a) *The New Meaning of Educational Change – Third Edition* London: RoutledgeFalmer

Fullan, M (2001b) *Leading in a Culture of Change* San Francisco: Jossey Bass

Fullan, M (2003) *Change Forces with a Vengeance* London: RoutledgeFalmer

Gardner, H (1985) *Frames of Mind: The Theory of Multiple Intelligences* London: Palladin Books

Gardner, H (1997) *Extraordinary Minds – Portraits of Exceptional Individuals and an Examination of Our Extraordinariness* London: Weidenfeld and Nicholson

Gillborn, D (1995) *Racism and Antiracism in Real Schools* Buckingham: Open University Press

Gillborn, D and Mirza, H (2000) *Educational Inequality: Mapping Race, Class and Gender, a Synthesis of Research Evidence* London: Ofsted

Gillborn, D and Youdell, D (2000) *Rationing Education: Policy, Practice, Reform and Equity* Buckingham: the Open University Press

Goleman, D (1996) *Emotional Intelligence – Why it can matter more than IQ* London: Bloomsbury

Goleman, D (2000) Leadership that gets Results *Harvard Business Review* September-October, p 78-90.

Gray, J, Hopkins, D, Reynolds, D, Wilcox, D, Farrell, S and Jesson, D (1999) *Improving Schools – Performance and Potential* Buckingham: Open University Press

Goldstein, H (2001) Review of 'Education and Social Justice' by Stephen Gorard *British Journal of Educational Studies* 49 (3), pages 354-357

Gorard, S (2000) *Education and Social Justice – The Changing Composition of Schools and its Implications* Cardiff: University of Wales Press

Gregory, E (Ed) (1997) *One Child, Many Worlds – Early Learning in Multicultural Communities* London: David Fulton

Haberman, M (1991) The Pedagogy of Poverty versus Good Teaching *Phi Delta Kappan* 73 (4) p290-4 Also reprinted in Ayers and Ford (1996)

Hallam, S (2002) *Ability Grouping in Schools* London: Institute of Education, University of London

Hallinger, P and Murphy, J (1986) The Social Context of Effective Schools *American Journal of Education* 94 (3), pages 328-355

Halsey, AH, Lauder, H, Brown, P and Stuart Wells, A (Eds) (1997) *Education – Culture, Economy and Society* Oxford: Oxford University Press.

Hopkins, D (2001) *School Improvement for Real* London: RoutledgeFalmer

Hopkins, D, Reynolds, D, Potter, D, Chapman, C together with Beresford, J, Jackson, P, Sharpe, T, Singleton, C and Watts, R (2001) *'Meeting the Challenge' – An Improvement Guide, a Handbook of Guidance and a Review of Research and Practice* London: DfEE

Howard, M, Garnham, A, Fimister, G and Veit-Wilson, J (2001) *Poverty: The Facts – 4th Edition* London: Child Poverty Action Group

Huberman, M (1983) Recipes for Busy Kitchens – A Situational Analysis of Routine Knowledge Use *Schools Knowledge: Creation, Diffusion, Utilisation* 4, p478-510

Jackson, B (1964) *Streaming – an Education System in Miniature* London: Routledge and Kegan Paul

Jackson, B and Marsden, D (1962) *Education and the Working Class* Harmondsworth: Penguin Books

Jensen, E (1995) *Super Teaching* San Diego, Ca: The Brain Store, Inc

Judge, H (1984) *A Generation of Schooling – English Secondary Schools since 1944* Oxford: Oxford University Press

Kounin, J (1970) *Discipline and Group Management in Classrooms* New York: Holt Rhinehart and Winston

Kozol, J (1991) *Savage Inequalities – Children in America's Schools* New York: Harper Perennial

Kozol, J (1995) *Amazing Grace – the Lives of Children and the Conscience of a Nation* New York: Harper Perennial

Mac an Ghaill, M (1988) *Young, Gifted and Black: Student-teacher Relations in the Schooling of Black Youth* Milton Keynes: Open University Press

McCulloch, G (2001) *The Reinvention of Teacher Professionalism* in Phillips and Furlong (Eds)

Major, J, Murray, O and Robins, J (1999) Identifying the Characteristics of Excellent Urban Teaching which Enable Teachers to Motivate Pupils and Enhance Their Engagement with Learning *Unpublished research report commissioned from trainee educational psychologists by Bristol LEA*

Miliband, D (2003) *Teaching in the 21st Century – Speech to the North of England Conference* London: DfES

Moll, L (Ed) (1992) *Vygotsky and Education – Instructional Implications and Applications of Sociohistorical Psychology* Cambridge: Cambridge University Press

Moll, L and Greenberg, J (1992) *Creating Zones of Possibilities: Combining Social Contexts for Instruction* in Moll, L *op cit* (Ed)

Morris, E (2002a) Speech to the Social Market Foundation From the DfES website – www.dfes.gov.uk

Morris, E (2002b) The London Challenge – speech made at South Community School on July 1st From the DfES website – www.dfes.gov.uk

Mortimore, P and Whitty, G (2000 edition) *Can School Improvement Overcome the Effects of Disadvantage?* London: Institute of Education, University of London

National Commission on Education (1993) *Learning to Succeed – a Radical Look at Education Today and A Strategy for the Future* London: Heinemann

NCSL (2002a) *Leading the Management of Change: Building Capacity for School Development* Nottingham: National College for School Leadership

NCSL (2002b) *Making the Difference: Successful Leadership in Challenging Circumstances – a Practical Guide to What Leaders Can Do to Energise Their Schools* Nottingham: National College for School Leadership

Newsam, P (1998) How Can We Know the Dancer From the Dance? *Forum* 40 (1) pages 4-10

Newsam, P (2002) Diversity and English Secondary Schools. Unpublished paper for the Secondary Heads' Association

Noden, P (2000) Rediscovering the impact of marketisation: dimensions of social segregation in England's Secondary Schools, 1994-99 *British Journal of Sociology of Education* 21 (3), pages 371-90

NRC (National Research Council) (1999) *Improving Student Learning: a Strategic Plan for Education Research and its Utilisation* Washington DC: National Academy Press

NRC (National Research Council) (2000) *How People Learn: Brain, Mind, Experience and School* Washington DC: National Academy Press

OECD (2001) *Knowledge and Skills for Life – First results form PISA 2000* Paris: Organisation for Economic Co-operation and Development

Ofsted (1993) *Access and Achievement in Urban Education* London: HMSO

Ofsted (1995) *Primary Matters – a Discussion on Teaching and Learning in Primary Schools* London: Ofsted

Ofsted (1999a) *Setting in Primary Schools* London: The Office of Her Majesty's Chief Inspector of Schools

Ofsted (1999b) *Handbook for Inspecting Primary and Nursery Schools with guidance on self-evaluation* London: The Stationery Office

Ofsted (2000a) *The National Numeracy Strategy: the First Year* London: Ofsted

Ofsted (2000b) *Improving City Schools – Strategies to Promote Educational Inclusion* London: Ofsted

Ofsted (2002a) *Standards and Quality in Education 2000/01 – the Annual Report of Her Majesty's Chief Inspector of Schools* London: The Stationery Office

Ofsted (2002b) *The Curriculum in Successful Primary Schools* London: Office for Standards in Education

Ofsted (2003) *Annual Report of Her Majesty's Chief Inspector of Schools: Standards and Quality in Education 2001/2* London: The Stationery Office

Osborn, M, McNess, E and Broadfoot, P with Pollard, A and Triggs, P (2000) *What Teachers Do – Changing Policy and Practice in Primary Education (Findings from the PACE Project)* London: Continuum

Pearce, N and Hillman, J (1998) *Wasted Youth – Raising Achievement and Tackling Social Exclusion* London: Institute for Public Policy Research

Phillips, R and Furlong, J (2001) *Education, Reform and the State – Twenty -Five Years of Politics, Policy and Practice* London: Routledge/Falmer

Pollard, A, Broadfoot, P, Croll, P, Osborn, M and Abbott, D (1994) *Changing English Primary Schools – The impact of the Education Reform Act at Key Stage 1* London: Cassell

Pollard, A with Filer, A (1996) *The Social World of Children's Learning – Case Studies of Pupils from Four to Seven* London: Cassell

Pollard, A and Triggs, P (2000) *What Pupils Say – Changing Policy and Practice in Primary Education (Findings from the PACE Project)* London: Continuum

Power, S, Warren, S, Gillborn, D, Clark, A, Thomas, S and Coate, K (2002) *Education in Deprived Areas – Outcomes, Inputs and Processes* London: Institute of Education

Reay, D (2002) Exclusivity, exclusion and social class in urban educational markets Paper presented at the British Educational Research Association conference Exeter, 2002

Reynolds, D (1998) Schooling for Literacy: review of the research *Education Review* 50 (2), pages 147-162

Reynolds, D and Farrell, S (1997) *Worlds Apart? A Review of International Surveys of Educational Achievement involving England* London: OFSTED

Roberts, K (2001) *Class in Modern Britain* Basingstoke: Palgrove

Rogers, B (2002) *Classroom Behaviour – a Practical Guide to Behaviour Management and Colleague Support* London: Paul Chapman Publishing

Rose, C and Nicholl, M (1997) *Accelerated Learning for the 21st Century* London: Piatkus

Rutter, M, Maugham, B, Mortimore, P and Ouston, J (1979) *Fifteen Thousand Hours – Secondary Schools and their Effects on Schoolchildren* Shepton Mallet: Open Books

Senge, P (1990) *The Fifth Discipline – the Art and Practice of the Learning Organisation* London: Century Business

Senge, P, Cambron-McCabe, N, Lucas, T, Smith, B, Dutton, J and Kleiner, A (2000) *Schools that Learn – A Fifth Discipline Fieldbook for Educators, Parents, and Everyone Who Cares About Education* London: Nicholas Brealey Publishing

Sewell, T (1997) *Black Masculinities and Schooling – How Black Boys Survive Modern Schooling* Stoke on Trent: Trentham Books

Slee, R and Weiner, G with Tomlinson, S (Eds) (1998) *School Effectiveness for Whom? Challenges to the School Effectiveness and School Improvement Movements* London: Falmer Press

Smith, A (1996) *Accelerated Learning in the Classroom* Stafford: Network Educational Press

Smithers, A and Robinson, P (2001) *Teachers Leaving* Liverpool: the Centre for Education and Employment Research, University of Liverpool

Social Exclusion Unit (1997) *Truancy and School Exclusion – A Report by the Social Exclusion Unit* London: The Stationery Office

Social Exclusion Unit (1999) *Bridging the Gap: New Opportunities for 16-18 Year Olds not in Education, Employment, or Training* London: The Stationery Office

Social Exclusion Unit (2001) *A New Commitment to Neighbourhood Renewal – National Strategy Action Plan* London: The Social Exclusion Unit

Stoll, L and Fink, D (1995) *Changing our Schools* Buckingham: Open University Press

Stoll, L and Myers, K (Eds) (1998) *No Quick Fixes – perspectives on schools in difficulty* London: Falmer Press

Stoll, L, Fink, D and Earl, L (2003) *It's About Learning (And It's About Time) – What's In It for Schools?* London: RoutledgeFalmer

Teddlie, C and Stringfield, S (1993) *Schools Make a Difference – Lessons Learned from a 10 Year Study* New York: Teachers College Press

Thomson, P (2002) *Schooling the Rustbelt Kids* Stoke on Trent: Trentham Books

Thrupp, M (1997) The School Mix Effect: How the Social Class Composition of School Intakes Shapes School Processes and Student Achievement. Paper presented to AERA Conference Chicago, March 1997

Thrupp, M (1999) *Schools Making A Difference: Let's be Realistic – School Mix, School Effectiveness and the Social Limits of Reform* Buckingham: Open University Press

Tizard, B, and Hughes, M (1984) *Young Children Learning – Talking and thinking at home and at school* London: Fontana Paperbacks

Tizard, B, Blatchford, P, Burke, J, Farquhar, C and Plewis, I (1988) *Young Children at School in the Inner City* London: Lawrence Erlbaum Associates

Tribal Education (2002) *Managing Multiple Initiatives – Final Report produced for Bristol Excellence in Cities* Bristol: Tribal

Twigg, S (2003) Letter to all primary headteachers Available on the DfES website, www.dfes.gov.uk

Tymms, P and Fitz-gibbon, C (2001) *Standards, Achievement and Educational Performance: a Cause for Celebration?* In Phillips and Furlong *op cit* (Eds)

Vincent, C (2002) *Parental Involvement and Voice in Inclusive Schooling* in Campbell *op cit* (Ed)

Vygotsky, L (1986) *Thought and Language* newly revised by A. Kozulin, Cambridge, Ma: The MIT Press

Whitty, G (2002) *Making Sense of Education Policy* London: Paul Chapman Publishers

Whitty, G, Power, S and Halpin, D (1998) *Devolution and Choice in Education – the School, the State and the Market* Buckingham: Open University Press

Wrigley, T (2000) *The Power to Learn – Stories of Success in the Education of Asian and other Bilingual Pupils* Stoke on Trent: Trentham Books

Index

476721

DH